Robert Rose's
Favorite

COOKIES
CAKES & PIES

Robert
ROSE

ROBERT ROSE'S FAVORITE COOKIES, CAKES & PIES

Canadian Cataloguing in Publication Data

Main entry under title:

Robert Rose's favorite cookies, cakes & pies

Includes index.

ISBN 1-896503-71-3

1. Cookies.   2. Cake   3. Pies.   I. Title: Favorite cookies, cakes & pies.

TX763.R62 1998   641.8'65   C98-931529-0

DESIGN AND PAGE COMPOSITION: MATTHEWS COMMUNICATIONS DESIGN
PHOTOGRAPHY: MARK T. SHAPIRO; RICHARD ALLEN
Cover photo: (DOUBLE CHOCOLATE CHUNK COOKIES, PAGE 15)

Distributed in the U.S. by: Distributed in Canada by:
Firefly Books (U.S.) Inc.   Stoddart Publishing Co. Ltd.
P.O. Box 1338   34 Lesmill Road
Ellicott Station   North York, Ontario
Buffalo, NY   14205   M3B 2T6

ORDER LINES	ORDER LINES
Tel: (416) 499-8412	Tel: (416) 213-1919
Fax: (416) 499-8313	Fax: (416) 213-1917

Published by: Robert Rose Inc. • 156 Duncan Mill Road, Suite 12
                 Toronto, Ontario, Canada M3B 2N2   Tel: (416) 449-3535

Printed in Canada   1234567 BP 01 00 99 98

About this book

At Robert Rose, we're committed to finding imaginative and exciting ways to provide our readers with cookbooks that offer great recipes — and exceptional value. That's the thinking behind our "Robert Rose's Favorite" series.

Here we present over 50 favorite recipes for cookies, cakes and pies — specially selected from a number of our bestselling full-sized cookbooks: Byron Ayanoglu's *New Vegetarian Gourmet* and *Simply Mediterranean Cooking*; Johanna Burkhard's *Comfort Food Cookbook* (plus several new cookie recipes from Johanna's kitchen); *New World Chinese Cooking*, by Bill Jones and Stephen Wong; and Rose Reisman's *Spa Desserts, Light Cooking, Enlightened Home Cooking* and *Light Vegetarian Cooking*. We've also included recipes from our own *Robert Rose Book of Classic Desserts*.

We believe that it all adds up to great value for anyone who loves cookies, cakes and pies.

Want to find out more about our books? See pages 94 and 95 for details.

Contents

Cookies

Cakes

Tarts and Pies

Other Desserts

Cookies

Makes about 4 dozen cookies

The secret to this tender shortbread is not to overwork the dough, especially when kneading. For light cookies, sift the flour, then spoon into metal measure; level top using a knife.

No-Fail Shortbread

PREHEAT OVEN TO 300° F (150° C)

1 cup	unsalted butter, softened	250 mL
1/2 cup	superfine sugar (fruit sugar)	125 mL
1 tsp	vanilla	5 mL
2 cups	sifted all-purpose flour	500 mL
1/4 tsp	salt	1 mL

1. In a bowl, beat butter with a wooden spoon until fluffy; beat in sugar a spoonful at time until well blended. Beat in vanilla. Stir in flour and salt; shape dough into a ball. On a lightly floured board, gently knead 4 to 5 times or until smooth.

2. Divide dough into 4 pieces. Roll each out on lightly floured surface to 1/3-inch (8 mm) thickness; cut out shapes using cookie cutters. Place on ungreased baking sheets. Bake, one sheet at a time, in middle of preheated oven for 25 to 30 minutes or until edges are light golden.

FROM
Johanna Burkhard

Rugelach
(Cinnamon Twist Chocolate Cookies)

PREHEAT OVEN TO 350° F (180° C)
BAKING SHEETS SPRAYED WITH VEGETABLE SPRAY

Dough

2 1/4 cups	all-purpose flour	550 mL
2/3 cup	granulated sugar	150 mL
1/2 cup	cold margarine *or* butter	125 mL
1/3 cup	2% yogurt	75 mL
3 to 4 tbsp	water	45 to 60 mL
1/2 cup	brown sugar	125 mL
1/3 cup	raisins	75 mL
2 tbsp	semi-sweet chocolate chips	25 mL
1 tbsp	cocoa	15 mL
1/2 tsp	cinnamon	2 mL

1. In a bowl combine flour and sugar. Cut in margarine until crumbly. Add yogurt and water; mix until combined. Roll into a smooth ball, wrap and place in refrigerator for 30 minutes.

2. Put brown sugar, raisins, chocolate chips, cocoa and cinnamon in food processor; process until crumbly, approximately 20 seconds.

3. Divide dough in half. Roll one portion into a rectangle of 1/4-inch (5 mm) thickness on a well-floured surface. Sprinkle half of the filling on top of the dough rectangle. Roll up tightly, long end to long end, jelly-roll fashion; pinch ends together. Cut into 1-inch (2.5 cm) thick pieces; some filling will fall out. Place on baking sheets cut side up. Repeat with remaining dough and filling.

4. With the back of a spoon or your fingers, gently flatten each cookie. Bake for 25 minutes, turning the cookies over at the halfway mark (12 1/2 minutes).

Makes about 32 cookies

Date Roll-Up Cookies

TIP

For maximum freshness, store cookies in airtight containers in the freezer; remove as needed.

Try this recipe with dried figs or apricots.

MAKE AHEAD

Prepare date mixture and freeze until needed.

PREHEAT OVEN TO 350° F (180° C)
LARGE BAKING SHEET SPRAYED WITH VEGETABLE SPRAY

Filling

8 oz	pitted dried dates	250 g
1 cup	orange juice	250 mL
1/4 tsp	ground cinnamon	1 mL

Dough

2 1/4 cups	all-purpose flour	550 mL
2/3 cup	granulated sugar	150 mL
1/4 cup	margarine *or* butter	50 mL
1/4 cup	vegetable oil	50 mL
1/4 cup	2% plain yogurt	50 mL
3 tbsp	water	45 mL
1 tsp	vanilla extract	5 mL
1 tsp	grated orange zest	5 mL

1. Make the filling: In a saucepan bring dates, orange juice and cinnamon to a boil; reduce heat to medium–low and cook 10 minutes or until soft. Mash with a fork until liquid is absorbed. Refrigerate.

2. Make the dough: In a food processor, combine flour, sugar, margarine, oil, yogurt, water, vanilla and orange zest; process until dough forms. Add up to 1 tbsp (15 mL) more water, if necessary. Divide dough in half; form each half into a ball, wrap and refrigerate for 15 minutes or until chilled.

3. Between 2 sheets of waxed paper sprinkled with flour, roll one of the dough balls into a rectangle, approximately 12 by 10 inches (30 by 25 cm) and 1/8 inch (5 mm) thick. Remove top sheet of waxed paper. Spread half of date mixture over rolled dough. Starting at short end and using the waxed paper as an aid, roll up tightly. Cut into 1/2-inch (1 cm) slices and place on prepared baking sheet. Repeat with remaining dough and filling.

4. Bake 25 minutes or until lightly browned.

FROM
Rose Reisman's Light
Vegetarian Cooking

Lemon Sugar Cookies

PREHEAT OVEN TO 350° F (180° C)

1 cup	unsalted butter, softened	250 mL
1 1/4 cups	granulated sugar	300 mL
2	whole eggs	2
1	egg yolk	1
1 tbsp	grated lemon rind	15 mL
3 cups	all-purpose flour	750 mL
1/2 tsp	baking powder	2 mL
1/2 tsp	salt	2 mL
1	egg white, lightly beaten	1
	Granulated sugar	

1. In a large bowl using an electric mixer, cream butter and sugar until light and fluffy. Beat in eggs, egg yolk and lemon rind until incorporated. In another bowl combine flour, baking powder and salt; stir into butter mixture to make a smooth dough. Place in plastic bag; refrigerate for 4 hours or overnight. (Dough can also be frozen for up to 1 month.)

2. Divide dough in half. On a floured board, roll each piece out to a scant 1/4-inch (5 mm) thickness. Cut out shapes using assorted cookie cutters; place on greased baking sheets. Lightly brush with egg white; using a small spoon sprinkle tops with a light coating of granulated sugar. Bake, one sheet at a time, in the middle of preheated oven for 12 to 14 minutes or until light golden around edges. Remove cookies to a rack to cool.

Makes about 6 dozen cookies

These crisp wafers are traditionally served with Glogg, a hot mulled wine, in Swedish homes at Christmas time. Here is a wonderful ritual carried on by many Swedish families, and which you may wish to adopt as part of your holiday traditions: Place a gingerbread in the palm of your hand and press in the center with one finger. The cookie should break into three (if not, eat that one and start again); then, without speaking, make a wish — and it will come true.

TIP

The secret to making crisp cookies is to roll dough out until very thin.

FROM
Johanna Burkhard

Swedish Ginger Wafers

2/3 cup	unsalted butter, softened	150 mL
1 cup	granulated sugar	250 mL
1/3 cup	corn syrup	75 mL
1/3 cup	water	75 mL
3 cups	all-purpose flour	750 mL
1 tsp	baking soda	5 mL
1 1/2 tsp	cinnamon	7 mL
3/4 tsp	ground cloves	4 mL
1/2 tsp	ground ginger	2 mL
1/2 tsp	ground cardamom (optional)	2 mL

1. In a large bowl using an electric mixer, cream butter with sugar until fluffy. In a small saucepan, bring corn syrup and water to a boil. Pour over creamed mixture and blend well. Sift flour with baking soda, cinnamon, cloves, ginger and cardamom. In three additions, stir dry ingredients into wet ingredients, stirring until well combined. Cover dough with plastic wrap and refrigerate at least 4 hours or overnight.

2. Remove dough from fridge and let stand at room temperature for 1 hour or until soft enough to roll out. Break off one-quarter of the dough and, on a floured surface, thinly roll out to scant 1/8-inch (3 mm) thickness. Using assorted cookie cutters, cut out shapes and place on parchment-lined or lightly greased baking sheets. Gather up scraps and reroll dough, using only enough flour to prevent the dough from sticking.

3. Bake cookies, one sheet at a time, in the middle of a preheated 400° F (200° C) oven for 5 to 6 minutes or until edges are lightly colored. Let cool on baking sheet for 1 minute, then remove to a rack to cool. Store cookies in a covered container in a cool dry place to maintain their crispness, or freeze.

**Makes
40 cookies**

TIP

The orange juice concentrate gives a more intense flavor than just orange juice. Remove some from package in freezer, then refreeze remainder.

If using bran flakes cereal, do not use All-Bran or raw bran.

Replace raisins with dried chopped dates, apricots or prunes.

MAKE AHEAD

Bake cookies up to a day ahead, keeping tightly covered in a cookie tin. Freeze cookie dough for up to 2 weeks.

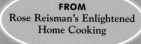

FROM
Rose Reisman's Enlightened
Home Cooking

Oatmeal Orange Coconut Cookies

PREHEAT OVEN TO 350° F (180° C)
BAKING SHEETS SPRAYED WITH VEGETABLE SPRAY

1/4 cup	margarine *or* butter	50 mL
1/4 cup	brown sugar	50 mL
1/2 cup	granualated sugar	125 mL
1	egg	1
1 tsp	vanilla	5 mL
2 tbsp	orange juice concentrate, thawed	25 mL
1/2 tsp	grated orange zest	2 mL
2/3 cup	all-purpose flour	150 mL
1/2 tsp	baking powder	2 mL
1/2 tsp	baking soda	2 mL
1/2 tsp	cinnamon	2 mL
1 cup	corn flakes *or* bran flakes cereal	250 mL
2/3 cup	raisins	150 mL
1/2 cup	rolled oats	125 mL
1/4 cup	coconut	50 mL

1. In a large bowl, cream together margarine, brown sugar and granulated sugar. Add egg, vanilla, orange juice concentrate and orange zest and mix well.

2. In another bowl, combine flour, baking powder, baking soda, cinnamon, corn flakes, raisins, rolled oats and coconut just until combined. Add to sugar mixture and mix until just combined

3. Drop by heaping teaspoons (5 mL) onto prepared baking sheets 2 inches (5 cm) apart and press down with back of fork; bake approximately 10 minutes or until browned.

**Makes 3 1/2
dozen cookies**

Double Chocolate Chunk Cookies

*Flecked with white
chocolate chunks
and walnuts, these
fudgy cookies are a
favorite with my fami-
ly. Served with a cold
glass of milk, they're
pure heaven. I'm
never short of taste
testers when the first
warm batch comes
from the oven.*

TIP

For perfectly baked
cookies, place baking
sheet on middle rack
of oven; do only one
sheet at time. Wipe
baking sheets with
paper towels or a
damp cloth to remove
grease. Let sheets
cool completely
before using again to
prevent dough from
melting and spread-
ing out too much
during baking.

❧

I like to double the
recipe, bake half and
freeze the remaining
dough to bake
another time.

❧

Nothing ruins a cook-
ie more than rancid
nuts, particularly wal-
nuts. Taste before pur-
chasing, if possible, to
make sure nuts are
fresh. Store them in a
covered container in
the fridge or freezer.

FROM
The Comfort Food Cookbook
by Johanna Burkhard

PREHEAT OVEN TO 350° F (180° C)

3/4 cup	granulated sugar	175 mL
1/2 cup	packed brown sugar	125 mL
2	large eggs	2
2 tsp	vanilla	10 mL
1 1/2 cups	all-purpose flour	375 mL
1/2 cup	cocoa powder	125 mL
1/2 tsp	baking soda	2 mL
1/2 tsp	salt	2 mL
1 1/2 cups	white chocolate chunks	375 mL
1 cup	chopped walnuts or pecans	250 mL

1. In a large bowl using an electric mixer, cream butter
with granulated and brown sugars until fluffy; beat in
eggs and vanilla until smooth.

2. In a separate bowl, sift together flour, cocoa powder,
baking soda and salt. Beat into creamed mixture until
combined; stir in white chocolate chunks and walnuts.

3. Drop tablespoonfuls (15 mL) of dough 2 inches (5 cm)
apart on ungreased baking sheets.

4. Bake in preheated oven for 10 to 12 minutes or until
edges are firm. (Bake for the shorter time if you prefer
cookies with a soft, chewy center.) Cool 2 minutes on
baking sheets; remove to wire rack and cool completely.

These crunchy morsels make wonderful gifts for friends and family. Pack biscotti in fancy containers or tins, or wrap in clear cellophane; decorate with a bright ribbon or bouquet of dried flowers.

TIP

Dried cranberries add a sweet-tart flavor; substitute golden raisins or chopped dried apricots, if desired.

Place hazelnuts on baking sheet in a 350° F (180° C) oven for 10 minutes or until lightly toasted. Place in clean dry towel and rub off most of the skins.

FROM
Johanna Burkhard

Hazelnut and Dried Cranberry Biscotti

PREHEAT OVEN TO 325° F (160° C)

1/2 cup	butter, softened	125 mL
1 cup	packed brown sugar	250 mL
2	large eggs	2
1 tsp	vanilla	5 mL
2 1/3 cups	all-purpose flour	575 mL
1 1/2 tsp	baking powder	7 mL
1 1/2 tsp	ground cinnamon	7 mL
1/4 tsp	ground cloves	1 mL
1/4 tsp	ground allspice	1 mL
1/4 tsp	salt	1 mL
1/2 cup	dried cranberries	125 mL
3/4 cup	hazelnuts, toasted and skinned, coarsely chopped	175 mL

1. In a large bowl using an electric mixer, cream butter and sugar until light and fluffy; beat in eggs and vanilla until smooth. In another bowl combine flour, baking powder, cinnamon, cloves, allspice and salt. Stir into creamed mixture to make a stiff dough. Stir in dried cranberries and hazelnuts.

2. With floured hands, divide dough in half. On a greased and floured baking sheet, pat into 2 logs, about 2 inches (5 cm) wide and 12 inches (30 cm) long, spacing about 2 inches (5 cm) apart. Bake in middle of preheated oven for 40 minutes or until golden brown and firm to the touch. Let cool 10 minutes. Using a long spatula, transfer to a cutting board. With a serrated knife, cut into 1/2-inch (1 cm) diagonal slices.

3. Place slices upright on baking sheet 1/2 inch (1 cm) apart and return to oven for 15 to 20 minutes longer or until crisp and dry. Let cool on rack. Store in a tightly covered container for up to 1 week, or freeze.

Istanbul Almond Cookies

*As a child in
Istanbul, if I was
particularly good,
my mother would
reward me with
some of these
cookies.
Practically butter-
less and flourless,
they were a lot
better for me than,
say, a piece of
chocolate — and
yet much more
satisfying. You can
turn these cookies
into a full-fledged
dessert by dress-
ing them with ice
cream and any
fruit sauce or
coulis, but they
remain great fun
just on their own.
Like all cookies,
they must be
stored in an
airtight container.*

**LARGE BAKING SHEET LINED WITH PARCHMENT PAPER
OR LARGE NONSTICK BAKING SHEET**

PREHEAT OVEN TO 350° F (180° C)

2 tbsp	unsalted butter, melted	25 mL
2	eggs, beaten	2
3/4 cup	granulated sugar	175 mL
1/4 tsp	almond extract	1 mL
2 cups	ground almonds	500 mL
1 tsp	baking powder	5 mL
24	whole blanched almonds	24

1. Brush baking sheet generously and thoroughly with butter.

2. In a bowl whisk together eggs, sugar and almond extract until pale yellow and smooth. Stir in ground almonds until well mixed, thick and sticky. Sprinkle with baking powder; stir until combined. Drop 4 tsp (20 mL) dollops of almond batter onto prepared baking sheet, spread about 1 inch (2.5 cm) apart. Place an almond on top of each cookie; push it into batter to embed it slightly.

3. Bake on the middle rack of oven for 18 to 20 minutes or until edges are brown. The cookies will spread out and touch one another as they bake. Cool for 10 minutes. With a knife, score to separate cookies; lift off with a spatula. Serve immediately while a little warm, or cool completely.

FROM
Simply Mediterranean Cooking
by Byron Ayanoglu and
Algis Kemezys

Makes 25 bars

Peanut Butter-Coconut-Raisin Granola Bars

TIP

Corn flakes can replace bran flakes. Don't worry if you only have Raisin Bran on hand.

Chopped dates can replace raisins.

Use a natural smooth or chunky peanut butter.

Do not overcook the peanut butter mixture.

MAKE AHEAD

Prepare these up to 2 days ahead and keep tightly closed in a cookie tin. These freeze for up to 2 weeks.

FROM
Rose Reisman's Enlightened
Home Cooking

PREHEAT OVEN TO 350° F (180° C)
9-INCH SQUARE (2.5 L) PAN SPRAYED WITH VEGETABLE SPRAY

1 1/3 cups	rolled oats	325 mL
2/3 cup	raisins	150 mL
1/2 cup	bran flakes	125 mL
1/3 cup	unsweetened coconut	75 mL
3 tbsp	chocolate chips	45 mL
2 tbsp	chopped pecans	25 mL
1 tsp	baking soda	5 mL
1/4 cup	peanut butter	50 mL
1/4 cup	brown sugar	50 mL
3 tbsp	margarine *or* butter	45 mL
3 tbsp	honey	45 mL
1 tsp	vanilla	5 mL

1. Put oats, raisins, bran flakes, coconut, chocolate chips, pecans and baking soda in bowl. Combine until well mixed.

2. In a small saucepan, whisk together peanut butter, brown sugar, margarine, honey and vanilla over medium heat for approximately 30 seconds or just until sugar dissolves and mixture is smooth. Pour over dry ingredients and stir to combine. Press into prepared pan and bake for 15 to 20 minutes or until browned. Let cool completely before cutting into bars.

Oatmeal Date Cookies

Makes 32 cookies

TIP

You can use Raisin Bran cereal. Do not use All-Bran or raw bran.

❧

Replace dates with dried apricots, prunes or raisins. Chop dried fruit with kitchen scissors.

❧

Keep dried fruits in freezer for maximum freshness.

MAKE AHEAD

Bake cookies up to a day ahead for best flavor, keeping tightly covered in cookie tin. Freeze cookie dough for up to 2 weeks.

❧

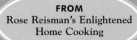

FROM
Rose Reisman's Enlightened
Home Cooking

PREHEAT OVEN TO 350° F (180° C)
BAKING SHEETS SPRAYED WITH VEGETABLE SPRAY

1/3 cup	margarine *or* butter	75 mL
1/3 cup	granulated sugar	75 mL
1	egg	1
1 tsp	vanilla	5 mL
2/3 cup	all–purpose flour	150 mL
1 tsp	baking powder	5 mL
3/4 tsp	cinnamon	4 mL
3/4 cup	rolled oats	175 mL
3/4 cup	bran flakes cereal *or* corn flakes	175 mL
2/3 cup	chopped pitted dried dates	150 mL

1. In a large bowl, cream together margarine and sugar. Add egg and vanilla; mix well.

2. In another bowl, combine flour, baking powder, cinnamon, rolled oats, cereal and dates. Add to sugar mixture and mix until just combined.

3. Drop by heaping teaspoonfuls (5 mL) onto prepared baking sheets 2 inches (5 cm) apart and press down with back of fork; bake for approximately 10 minutes or until browned.

Gingersnaps

A favorite since my university days, these spice cookies would provide fuel for cram sessions before exams. Now, continuing the tradition, I bake a batch when my kids have to hit the books.

TIP

Be sure to use fresh baking soda as it makes cookies crisp and light.

Like baking powder, an open box of baking soda has a shelf life of only 6 months, so make sure to replenish both regularly. As a reminder, write the date when they need to be replaced on the container.

PREHEAT OVEN TO 350° F (180° C)
BAKING SHEET(S), LIGHTLY GREASED

1/2 cup	shortening, softened	125 mL
1/2 cup	butter, softened	125 mL
3/4 cup	packed brown sugar	175 mL
1/4 cup	molasses	50 mL
1	large egg, beaten	1
2 1/4 cups	all-purpose flour	550 mL
1 1/2 tsp	baking soda	7 mL
1 1/2 tsp	ground ginger	7 mL
1 tsp	ground cinnamon	5 mL
1 tsp	ground cloves	5 mL
1/4 tsp	salt	1 mL
	Granulated sugar	

1. In a large bowl, cream shortening and butter with sugar until light and fluffy; beat in molasses and egg until creamy.

2. In another bowl, sift together flour, baking soda, ginger, cinnamon, ground cloves and salt. Stir into creamed mixture to make a soft dough. Refrigerate for 1 hour or until firm.

3. Shape dough into 1-inch (2.5 cm) balls; roll in bowl of granulated sugar. Arrange 2 inches (5 cm) apart on prepared baking sheets. Flatten to 1/4 inch (5 mm) thickness using bottom of large glass dipped in sugar.

4. Bake in preheated oven for 12 to 14 minutes or until golden. Cool 2 minutes on baking sheets; transfer to rack and let cool.

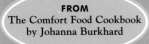

FROM
The Comfort Food Cookbook
by Johanna Burkhard

Makes 45 cookies

TIP

Use almonds, hazelnuts, pine nuts or a combination.

MAKE AHEAD

Store in airtight container up to 2 weeks, or freeze for up to 1 month.

FROM
Rose Reisman Brings Home
Light Cooking

Pecan Biscotti

PREHEAT OVEN TO 350° F (180° C)
BAKING SHEET SPRAYED WITH VEGETABLE SPRAY

2	eggs	2
3/4 cup	granulated sugar	175 mL
1/3 cup	margarine	75 mL
1/4 cup	water	50 mL
2 tsp	vanilla	10 mL
1 tsp	almond extract	5 mL
2 3/4 cups	all-purpose flour	675 mL
1/2 cup	chopped pecans	125 mL
2 1/4 tsp	baking powder	11 mL

1. In a large bowl, blend eggs with sugar; beat in margarine, water, vanilla and almond extract until smooth.

2. Add flour, pecans and baking powder; mix until dough forms ball. Divide dough in half; shape each portion into a log 12 inches (30 cm) long and place on baking sheet. Bake for 20 minutes. Let cool for 5 minutes.

3. Cut logs diagonally into 1/2-inch (1 cm) thick slices. Place slices on sides on baking sheet; bake for 20 minutes or until lightly browned.

Makes 40 cookies

Peanut Butter Chocolate Chip Cookies

TIP

The longer they bake, the crisper the cookies.

Nuts can replace the raisins.

Use natural peanut butter made from only peanuts.

MAKE AHEAD

Dough can be frozen up to 2 weeks. Bake just before eating for best flavor.

FROM
Rose Reisman Brings Home
Light Cooking

PREHEAT OVEN TO 350° F (180° C)
BAKING SHEETS SPRAYED WITH VEGETABLE SPRAY

1/2 cup	brown sugar	125 mL
1/3 cup	granulated sugar	75 mL
1/3 cup	peanut butter	75 mL
1/3 cup	2% milk	75 mL
1/4 cup	soft margarine	50 mL
1	egg	1
1 tsp	vanilla	5 mL
1/2 cup	all-purpose flour	125 mL
1/3 cup	whole wheat flour	75 mL
1 tsp	baking soda	5 mL
1/3 cup	chocolate chips	75 mL
1/4 cup	raisins	50 mL

1. In a large bowl or food processor, beat together brown and granulated sugars, peanut butter, milk, margarine, egg and vanilla until well blended.

2. Combine all-purpose and whole wheat flours and baking soda; add to bowl and mix just until incorporated. Do not overmix. Stir in chocolate chips and raisins.

3. Drop by heaping teaspoonfuls (5 mL) 2 inches (5 cm) apart onto baking sheets. Bake for 12 to 15 minutes or until browned.

Cakes

Serves 8 to 10

Nothing is more seductive than crimson strawberries, cold whipped cream and buttery-lemon cake. For me, this perfect summer dessert beats out shortcake hands down as the ultimate strawberry creation.

TIP

Strawberries can be replaced with other small fruits such as raspberries, blueberries or blackberries. Or use a combination of several berries.

To make your own superfine sugar, place granulated sugar in a food processor; process until very fine.

For fluffy whipped cream, make sure the cream is very cold before beating. As well, place the beaters and bowl in the freezer for 10 minutes before you start.

FROM
The Comfort Food Cookbook
by Johanna Burkhard

Strawberry Cream Cake

PREHEAT OVEN TO 350° F (180° C)
9-INCH (23 CM) SPRINGFORM PAN, GREASED AND FLOURED

Sponge Cake

3	large eggs	3
1 cup	granulated sugar	250 mL
1 1/2 cups	all-purpose flour	375 mL
2 tsp	baking powder	10 mL
1/4 tsp	salt	1 mL
3/4 cup	milk	175 mL
1/3 cup	butter, melted	75 mL
1 tsp	grated lemon zest	5 mL

Filling

1 1/2 cups	whipping (35%) cream	375 mL
1 tsp	vanilla	5 mL
1/4 cup	superfine sugar	50 mL
3 cups	sliced strawberries	750 mL
1 cup	whole small strawberries	250 mL
	Mint sprigs	

1. In a mixing bowl using an electric mixer at high speed, beat eggs and sugar for 3 minutes or until thick and creamy.

2. In a separate bowl, combine flour, baking powder and salt. In a glass measuring cup, combine milk, melted butter and lemon zest.

3. Beat dry ingredients into egg mixture alternately with milk mixture until batter is just smooth.

4. Pour into prepared pan. Bake in preheated oven for 35 minutes or until cake tester inserted in center comes out clean.

5. Let cake cool for 5 minutes; run knife around edge and remove sides. Place on rack to cool completely. Using a long serrated knife, slice cake horizontally to make 3 layers each about 1/2 inch (1 cm) thick.

6. In a bowl with an electric mixer, whip cream until soft peaks form. Beat in vanilla and sugar, a spoonful (5 mL) at a time, until stiff peaks form.

7. Arrange 1 cake layer, cut-side up on a large serving plate. Spread with one-third of the whipped cream; top with half the sliced berries, including some juice. Arrange second cake layer on top. Spread with one-third of the whipped cream and remaining sliced berries with juice. Arrange third layer on top; spread top with remaining whipped cream. Garnish with small whole berries and mint sprigs.

Carrot Cake with Cream Cheese Frosting

PREHEAT OVEN TO 350° F (180° C)
9-INCH (3 L) BUNDT PAN SPRAYED WITH VEGETABLE SPRAY

1/3 cup	margarine *or* butter	75 mL
1 cup	granulated sugar	250 mL
2	eggs	2
1 tsp	vanilla	5 mL
1	large ripe banana, mashed	1
2 cups	grated carrots	500 mL
2/3 cup	raisins	150 mL
1/2 cup	canned pineapple, drained and crushed	125 mL
1/2 cup	2% yogurt	125 mL
2 cups	all-purpose flour	500 mL
1 1/2 tsp	baking powder	7 mL
1 1/2 tsp	baking soda	7 mL
1 1/2 tsp	cinnamon	7 mL
1/4 tsp	nutmeg	1 mL

Icing

1/3 cup	light cream cheese, softened	75 mL
2/3 cup	icing sugar	150 mL
1 tbsp	2% milk	15 mL

1. In a large bowl, cream together margarine and sugar until smooth; add eggs and vanilla and beat well (mixture may look curdled). Add mashed banana, carrots, raisins, pineapple and yogurt; stir until well combined.

2. In a bowl stir together flour, baking powder, baking soda, cinnamon and nutmeg. Add to the carrot mixture; stir just until combined. Pour into prepared pan and bake for 40 to 45 minutes or until cake tester inserted in the center comes out clean. Let cool for 10 minutes before inverting onto serving plate.

3. In a bowl or food processor, beat together cream cheese, icing sugar and milk until smooth; drizzle over top of cake. Decorate with grated carrots if desired.

Serves 6 to 8

FROM
The Robert Rose Book
of Classic Desserts

Strawberry Cream Dacquoise (Boccone Dolce)

PREHEAT OVEN TO 275° F (140° C)
3 BAKING SHEETS LINED WITH PARCHMENT PAPER

Meringue

1 cup	egg whites (about 7 egg whites)	250 mL
1/4 tsp	cream of tartar	1 mL
2 cups	granulated sugar	500 mL

Filling

4 oz	semi-sweet chocolate, chopped	125 g
2 tbsp	water	25 mL
3 cups	whipping (35%) cream	750 mL
1/3 cup	sifted icing sugar	75 mL
2 1/4 cups	strawberries, sliced	550 mL

1. Using the base of an 8-inch (2 L) springform pan as a template, draw an 8-inch (20 cm) circle on each parchment-lined baking sheet. Butter and flour parchment paper.

2. Make the meringue: In a bowl, beat egg whites with cream of tartar until soft peaks form; gradually add sugar, beating until glossy, stiff peaks form. Spoon meringue onto circles on parchment paper, or pipe onto circles using a pastry bag. Bake 1 1/2 to 3 hours or until meringue is golden. Cool on wire racks.

3. Make the filling: In a bowl, melt the chocolate over hot (not boiling) water, stirring until smooth; set aside. In another bowl, whip cream until it starts to thicken; gradually add icing sugar, beating until stiff peaks form.

4. Assembly: Put 1 meringue circle on serving platter; spread with melted chocolate (reheat chocolate if too thick). Spread with whipped cream to 3/4-inch (2 cm) thickness; top with sliced strawberries. Repeat. Top with last meringue circle; ice top and sides with remaining whipped cream. Decorate with remaining strawberries and drizzle with remaining chocolate. Chill 2 hours before serving.

Sardi's — New York

Makes 16 slices

TIP

If using frozen blueberries, thaw first; then drain off the excess liquid.

Apples or pears are good substitutes for the peaches.

MAKE AHEAD

Bake a day before or freeze for up to 6 weeks.

FROM
Rose Reisman Brings Home
Light Cooking

Blueberry Peach Cake

PREHEAT OVEN TO 350° F (180° C)
9-INCH (3 L) BUNDT PAN SPRAYED WITH VEGETABLE SPRAY

1 cup	granulated sugar	250 mL
3/4 cup	applesauce	175 mL
1/4 cup	vegetable oil	50 mL
2	eggs	2
1 tsp	vanilla	5 mL
1 1/2 cups	all-purpose flour	375 mL
1/2 cup	whole wheat flour	125 mL
2 tsp	cinnamon	10 mL
1 1/2 tsp	baking powder	7 mL
1 tsp	baking soda	5 mL
1/2 cup	2% yogurt	125 mL
1 cup	sliced peeled peaches	250 mL
1 cup	blueberries	250 mL
	Icing sugar	

1. In a large bowl, beat together sugar, applesauce, oil, eggs and vanilla, mixing well.

2. Combine all-purpose and whole wheat flours, cinnamon, baking powder and baking soda; stir into bowl just until blended. Stir in yogurt; fold in peaches and blueberries. Pour into pan.

3. Bake for 40 to 45 minutes or until cake tester inserted into centre comes out clean. Let cool; dust with icing sugar.

Date Cake with Coconut Topping

TIP

To chop dates easily, use kitchen shears. Whole pitted dates can be used, but then use food processor to finely chop dates after they are cooked.

Chopped pitted prunes can replace dates.

MAKE AHEAD

Prepare up to 2 days ahead, or freeze for up to 6 weeks. The dates keep this cake moist.

FROM
Rose Reisman's Enlightened
Home Cooking

PREHEAT OVEN TO 350° F (180° C)
9-INCH SQUARE (2.5 L) CAKE PAN SPRAYED WITH VEGETABLE SPRAY

Cake

12 oz	pitted dried dates, chopped	300 g
1 3/4 cups	water	425 mL
1/4 cup	margarine *or* butter	50 mL
1 cup	granulated sugar	250 mL
2	eggs	2
1 1/2 cups	all-purpose flour	375 mL
1 1/2 tsp	baking powder	7 mL
1 tsp	baking soda	5 mL

Topping

1/3 cup	unsweetened coconut	75 mL
1/4 cup	brown sugar	50 mL
3 tbsp	2% milk	45 mL
2 tbsp	margarine *or* butter	25 mL

1. Put dates and water in a saucepan; bring to a boil, cover and reduce heat to low. Cook for 10 minutes, stirring often, or until dates are soft and most of the liquid has been absorbed. Set aside to cool for 10 minutes.

2. In a large bowl or food processor, beat together margarine and sugar. Add eggs and mix well. Add cooled date mixture and mix well.

3. In a bowl combine flour, baking powder and baking soda. Stir into date mixture just until blended. Pour into cake pan and bake for 35 to 40 minutes or until cake tester inserted in center comes out dry.

4. In a small saucepan, combine coconut, brown sugar, milk and margarine; cook over medium heat, stirring, for 2 minutes or until sugar dissolves. Pour over cake.

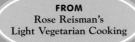

FROM
Rose Reisman's
Light Vegetarian Cooking

Sour Cream Orange Apple Cake

PREHEAT OVEN TO 350° F (180° C)
10-INCH (3 L) SPRINGFORM PAN SPRAYED WITH VEGETABLE SPRAY

Topping

1/3 cup	packed brown sugar	75 mL
3 tbsp	chopped pecans	45 mL
1 1/2 tbsp	all-purpose flour	20 mL
2 tsp	margarine *or* butter	10 mL
1/2 tsp	ground cinnamon	2 mL

Filling

2 cups	chopped peeled apples	500 mL
1/2 cup	raisins	125 mL
1 tbsp	granulated sugar	15 mL
1 tsp	ground cinnamon	5 mL

Cake

2/3 cup	packed brown sugar	150 mL
1/2 cup	granulated sugar	125 mL
1/3 cup	vegetable oil	75 mL
2	eggs	2
1 tbsp	grated orange zest	15 mL
2 tsp	vanilla extract	10 mL
1 2/3 cups	all-purpose flour	400 mL
2 tsp	baking powder	10 mL
1 tsp	baking soda	5 mL
1/2 cup	orange juice	125 mL
1/2 cup	light sour cream	125 mL

1. Make the topping: In a small bowl, combine brown sugar, pecans, flour, margarine and cinnamon. Set aside.

2. Make the filling: In a bowl mix together apples, raisins, sugar and cinnamon. Set aside.

3. Make the cake: In a food processor or in a large bowl with an electric mixer, beat together brown sugar, granulated sugar and oil Add eggs, one at a time, beating well after each. Mix in orange zest and vanilla.

4. In a separate bowl, stir together flour, baking powder and baking soda. In another bowl, stir together orange juice and sour cream. Add flour mixture and sour cream mixture alternately to beaten sugar mixture, mixing just until blended. Spoon half of batter into prepared pan. Top with half of apple mixture. Spoon remaining batter into pan. Top with remaining apple mixture; sprinkle with topping.

5. Bake 45 to 50 minutes, or until cake tester inserted in center comes out clean. Cool on a wire rack.

Apple Pecan Streusel Cake

PREHEAT OVEN TO 350° F (180° C)
9-INCH (3 L) BUNDT PAN SPRAYED WITH VEGETABLE SPRAY

1/4 cup	soft margarine	50 mL
1 cup	brown sugar	250 mL
2	eggs	2
2 tsp	vanilla	10 mL
1 1/4 cups	all-purpose flour	300 mL
3/4 cup	whole wheat flour	175 mL
2 1/2 tsp	cinnamon	12 mL
1 1/2 tsp	baking powder	7 mL
1 tsp	baking soda	5 mL
1 cup	2% yogurt *or* light sour cream	250 mL
2 3/4 cups	diced peeled apples	675 mL
1/4 cup	raisins	50 mL

Topping

1/4 cup	chopped pecans	50 mL
1/4 cup	all-purpose flour	50 mL
3 tbsp	brown sugar	45 mL
1 tbsp	margarine, melted	15 mL
1 1/2 tsp	cinnamon	7 mL

1. Topping: In a small bowl, combine pecans, flour, sugar, margarine and cinnamon until crumbly. Set aside.

2. In a large bowl or food processor, cream together margarine and sugar. Beat in eggs and vanilla until well blended.

3. Combine all-purpose and whole wheat flours, cinnamon, baking powder and baking soda; add to bowl alternately with yogurt, mixing just until blended. Fold in apples and raisins. Pour into pan.

4. Sprinkle with topping; bake for 40 to 45 minutes or until cake tester inserted into center comes out clean.

Sour Cream Cinnamon Coffee Cake

PREHEAT OVEN TO 350° F (180° C)
8.5-INCH (2.25 L) SPRINGFORM PAN SPRAYED WITH
VEGETABLE SPRAY

Cake

1/3 cup	margarine *or* butter	75 mL
2/3 cup	granulated sugar	150 mL
2	eggs	2
1 tsp	vanilla	5 mL
1 1/4 cups	all-purpose flour	300 mL
1 1/2 tsp	baking powder	7 mL
1 1/4 tsp	cinnamon	6 mL
1/2 tsp	baking soda	2 mL
1 cup	light sour cream *or* 2% yogurt	250 mL

Filling

2/3 cup	brown sugar	150 mL
1/2 cup	raisins	125 mL
3 tbsp	semi-sweet chocolate chips	45 mL
4 1/2 tsp	cocoa	22 mL
1/2 tsp	cinnamon	2 mL

1. In a large bowl, cream together margarine and sugar; add eggs and vanilla and mix well. In a bowl combine flour, baking powder, cinnamon and baking soda; stir into wet ingredients alternately with sour cream just until mixed.

2. Put brown sugar, raisins, chocolate chips, cocoa and cinnamon in food processor; process until crumbly.

3. Put half of batter into prepared pan; top with half of filling. Repeat layers. Bake for approximately 40 minutes or until cake tester inserted in the center comes out clean.

Serves 14 to 16

Cointreau Chocolate Decadence

FROM
The Robert Rose Book
of Classic Desserts

10- TO 12-INCH (3 TO 4 L) SPRINGFORM PAN

Crust

1 cup	chocolate wafer crumbs	250 mL
3 tbsp	melted butter	45 mL

Filling

1 lb	semi-sweet chocolate, chopped	500 g
10	egg yolks	10
1/3 cup	granulated sugar	75 mL
1	pkg (1 tbsp [7 g]) gelatin	1
1/3 cup	Cointreau *or* other orange flavored liqueur	75 mL
2 1/2 cups	whipping (35%) cream	625 mL

Ganache

12 oz	semi-sweet chocolate, chopped	375 g
3/4 cup	whipping (35%) cream	175 mL
	Large chocolate curls (optional)	

1. Make the crust: In a bowl combine chocolate wafer crumbs and melted butter. Pat onto bottom of pan. Chill while making filling.

2. Make the filling: In a bowl melt chocolate over hot (not boiling) water, stirring until smooth; cool slightly. In another bowl, beat egg yolks and sugar until pale yellow and thick; beat in chocolate until blended. Dissolve gelatin in water according to package directions; stir into chocolate mixture. In a separate bowl, whip cream until stiff peaks form; fold gently into chocolate mixture. Pour into crust. Freeze until the top is set.

3. Make the ganache: In a bowl, melt chocolate over hot (not boiling) water, stirring until smooth; cool slightly. Slowly beat in cream. If ganache hardens before use, reheat slightly until it is of spreading consistency; if ganache is not stiff enough to glaze, chill for a short time.

4. Assembly: Unmold dessert; transfer to a serving platter. Glaze top and sides with ganache. Decorate with large chocolate curls, if desired.

Inn on the Park — Toronto

TIP

After frosting the cake, decorate it with toasted coconut or toasted nuts for a special presentation.

FROM
The Robert Rose Book
of Classic Desserts

Old-Fashioned Carrot Cake

PREHEAT OVEN TO 350° F (180° C)
TWO 9-INCH (1.5 L) ROUND CAKE PANS, BUTTERED AND FLOURED

Cake

4	eggs	4
1 1/2 cups	granulated sugar	375 mL
1 1/2 cups	vegetable oil	375 mL
1 cup	all-purpose flour	250 mL
1 cup	cake and pastry flour	250 mL
2 tsp	baking powder	10 mL
2 tsp	cinnamon	10 mL
1 tsp	baking soda	5 mL
3 cups	grated carrots	750 mL
1 1/2 cups	chopped walnuts	375 mL
1 cup	raisins	250 mL

Old-Fashioned Butter Cream Cheese Icing

2	egg whites	2
1 1/4 cups	icing sugar	300 mL
2/3 cup	butter, softened	150 mL
1/2 cup	vegetable shortening	125 mL
4 oz	cream cheese, softened	125 g
1/2 tsp	vanilla extract	2 mL

1. Make the cake: In a large bowl, beat eggs; beat in sugar and oil until blended. In another bowl, sift together flour, cake flour, baking powder, cinnamon and baking soda; with a wooden spoon, stir into wet ingredients just until blended. Do not overmix. Fold in carrots, walnuts and raisins. Divide between prepared cake pans. Bake 35 to 40 minutes or until cake tester inserted in center comes out clean. Cool in pans on wire rack.

2. Make the icing: In a bowl, beat egg whites until stiff peaks form; beat in icing sugar. Beat in butter and shortening until well-mixed. Beat in cream cheese and vanilla until smooth.

3. Invert cooled cakes. Put one cake layer on serving platter. Spread top with icing. Top with other cake layer. Spread icing over top and sides of cake.

Dessert Peddler – Toronto

Glazed Espresso Chocolate Cake

TIP

To make coffee quickly, dissolve 1 tsp (5 mL) instant coffee granules in 1/2 cup (125 mL) boiling water. Use decaffeinated if desired.

You can also make muffins with this recipe; just pour batter into 12 cups and bake for approximately 20 minutes.

This cake is also excellent without the glaze.

MAKE AHEAD

Freeze without glaze for up to 2 weeks.

PREHEAT OVEN TO 350° F (180° C)
8-INCH (2 L) SPRINGFORM PAN SPRAYED WITH VEGETABLE SPRAY

1/2 cup	brown sugar	125 mL
1/2 cup	granulated sugar	125 mL
1/3 cup	margarine	75 mL
2	eggs	2
1 tsp	vanilla	5 mL
1/4 cup	unsweetened cocoa powder	50 mL
1 cup	all-purpose flour	250 mL
1 tsp	baking soda	5 mL
1 tsp	baking powder	5 mL
1/2 cup	hot strong coffee	125 mL
1/3 cup	low-fat yogurt *or* buttermilk	75 mL

Glaze

1 cup	icing sugar	250 mL
2 tbsp	strong coffee	25 mL
	Unsweetened cocoa powder	

1. In a large bowl or food processor, beat together brown and granulated sugars, margarine, eggs and vanilla until well blended. Add cocoa and mix until well incorporated.

2. Combine flour, baking soda and baking powder; add to bowl along with coffee and yogurt. Mix just until combined, being careful not to overmix. Pour into pan; bake for 35 to 40 minutes or until tester inserted into center comes out dry. Let cool completely.

3. Glaze: In a small bowl, mix icing sugar with coffee until smooth, adding more coffee if too thick. Spread over cake, smoothing with knife. Sift cocoa over top to decorate.

Serves 12

Double Chocolate Chip Banana Cake

PREHEAT OVEN TO 350° F (180° C)
12-CUP (3 L) BUNDT PAN

1 cup	packed brown sugar	250 mL
1/2 cup	granulated sugar	125 mL
1/3 cup	vegetable oil	75 mL
1	ripe medium banana, mashed	1
1 tsp	vanilla extract	5 mL
2	eggs	2
2 cups	finely chopped or grated peeled zucchini *or* carrots (about 8 oz [250 g])	500 mL
1/2 cup	canned crushed pineapple	125 mL
2 cups	all-purpose flour	500 mL
1/3 cup	cocoa	75 mL
1 1/2 tsp	baking powder	7 mL
1 1/2 tsp	baking soda	7 mL
1/3 cup	semi-sweet chocolate chips	75 mL
1/4 cup	light sour cream	50 mL

Chocolate Cream Cheese Icing

1/3 cup	light cream cheese, softened	75 mL
1 cup	icing sugar	250 mL
1 tbsp	cocoa	15 mL
1 tbsp	2% milk	15 mL

1. In a food processor, combine brown sugar, granulated sugar, oil, banana, vanilla and eggs; process until smooth. Add zucchini and pineapple; process just until combined.

2. In a bowl stir together flour, cocoa, baking powder and baking soda. Stir wet ingredients into dry ingredients just until mixed. Stir in chocolate chips and sour cream. Spoon into prepared pan. Bake 40 to 45 minutes or until tester inserted in center comes out clean. Let cool.

3. With an electric mixer, cream together cream cheese, icing sugar, cocoa and milk. Spread over cooled cake.

TIP

The surprise ingredient here is zucchini, which gives incredible moisture to the cake. If zucchini is not available, substitute carrots.

Freeze overripe bananas in their skins up to 3 months. Defrost and use mashed in baking.

Leave out the icing if you wish — but it is delicious!

MAKE AHEAD

Bake up to 2 days in advance.

Freeze tightly wrapped for up to 6 weeks.

FROM
Rose Reisman's Light Vegetarian Cooking

Serves 12

TIP

It's easier to separate eggs when they're cold.

Egg whites beat to a greater volume when at room temperature.

White and Dark Chocolate Marbled Mousse Cake

12-INCH (4 L) SPRINGFORM PAN

Crust

1 cup	chocolate wafer crumbs	250 mL
3 tbsp	melted butter	45 mL

Chocolate filling

14 oz	semi-sweet chocolate, chopped	425 g
2	eggs	2
4	eggs, separated	4
2 cups	whipping (35%) cream	500 mL

White Chocolate Mousse

2 1/2 oz	white chocolate	75 g
2	eggs, separated	2
1/2 cup	whipping (35%) cream	125 mL

1. Make the crust: In a bowl combine chocolate wafer crumbs and melted butter. Pat onto bottom of pan. Chill while preparing filling.

2. Make the chocolate filling: In a bowl, melt the chocolate over hot (not boiling) water, stirring until smooth; remove from heat. Beat in eggs and egg yolks. In another bowl, beat egg whites until stiff peaks form. In a separate bowl, whip cream until soft peaks form. Alternately fold whites and whipped cream into chocolate mixture. Pour into crust; set aside.

3. Make the chocolate mousse: In a bowl, melt the white chocolate over hot (not boiling) water, stirring until smooth; remove from heat. Beat in egg yolks. In another bowl, beat egg whites until stiff peaks form. In a separate bowl, whip cream until soft peaks form. Alternately fold whites and whipped cream into white chocolate mixture. Pour into center of dark chocolate mousse. With a knife, swirl white mousse through dark mousse. Chill 3 to 4 hours before serving.

FROM
The Robert Rose Book of Classic Desserts

The Quilted Giraffe – New York

Serves 8 to 10

TIP

Use clean beaters and bowl when beating egg whites.

White Chocolate Mousse Layer Cake with Raspberries

PREHEAT OVEN TO 350° F (180° C)
9-INCH (2.5 L) SPRINGFORM PAN, BUTTERED AND FLOURED

Chocolate Sponge

3	eggs, separated	3
1/2 cup	granulated sugar	125 mL
1 tsp	vanilla extract	5 mL
1 1/2 tbsp	cocoa	22 mL
1 tbsp	all-purpose flour	15 mL

White Chocolate Mousse

10 oz	white chocolate, chopped	300 g
3	eggs, separated	3
1 1/2 cups	whipping (35%) cream	375 mL
1 tbsp	granulated sugar	15 mL
2 1/4 cups	raspberries	550 mL
	White chocolate shavings (optional)	

1. Make the chocolate sponge: In a bowl, beat egg yolks with 1/4 cup (50 mL) of the sugar until pale yellow and thick; beat in vanilla. Gently fold in cocoa and flour; set aside. In another bowl, beat egg whites until soft peaks form; gradually add remaining sugar, beating until stiff peaks form. Fold egg whites into batter. Pour into prepared pan. Bake 20 minutes or until cake tester inserted in center comes out clean. Cool in pan on wire rack.

2. Make the white chocolate mousse: In a bowl, melt chocolate over hot (not boiling) water, stirring until smooth; cool slightly. Beat egg yolks; blend into chocolate and set aside. In a bowl whip cream until soft peaks form. In another bowl, beat egg whites until soft peaks form; gradually add sugar, beating, until stiff peaks form. Stir one-quarter of egg whites into chocolate mixture to lighten; gently fold in remaining egg whites and whipped cream.

FROM
The Robert Rose Book
of Classic Desserts

3. Assembly: Remove ring of springform pan. Cut cake horizontally into 2 layers; remove top layer and replace ring. Pour one-third of mousse over bottom layer; scatter half the raspberries on top. Top with other cake layer. Pour one-third mousse over bottom layer; scatter half the raspberries on top. Top with other cake layer. Pour one-third of mousse on top. Chill cake and remaining mousse for at least 2 hours.

4. To serve, unmold cake and spread sides with remaining mousse. Decorate with remaining raspberries and white chocolate shavings, if desired.

Tavern on the Green – New York

Cheesecakes

Chocolate Cheesecake with Sour Cream Topping

PREHEAT OVEN TO 350° F (180° C)
8-INCH (2 L) SPRINGFORM PAN SPRAYED WITH VEGETABLE SPRAY

8 oz	ricotta cheese	250 g
8 oz	2% cottage cheese	250 g
1 cup	granulated sugar	250 mL
1	large egg	1
1 tsp	vanilla	5 mL
1/4 cup	sifted unsweetened cocoa powder	50 mL
1 tbsp	all-purpose flour	15 mL
Crust		
1 1/2 cups	graham or chocolate wafer crumbs	375 mL
2 tbsp	water	25 mL
1 tbsp	margarine, melted	15 mL
Topping		
1 cup	light sour cream	250 mL
2 tbsp	granulated sugar	25 mL
1 tsp	vanilla	5 mL

1. Crust: In a bowl combine crumbs, water and margarine; mix well. Pat onto bottom and sides of springform pan. Refrigerate.

2. In a food processor, combine ricotta and cottage cheeses, sugar, egg and vanilla; process until smooth. Add cocoa and flour; process just until combined. Pour into pan and bake for 30 minutes or until set around edge but still slightly loose in center.

3. Topping: Meanwhile, stir together sour cream, sugar and vanilla; pour over cheesecake. Bake for 10 more minutes. (Topping will be loose.) Let cool and refrigerate for at least 3 hours or until set.

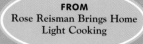

FROM
Rose Reisman Brings Home
Light Cooking

Serves 8 to 10

TIP

Use extra smooth ricotta for the smoothest-textured cheesecake.

FROM
The Robert Rose Book of Classic Desserts

Almond Ricotta Cheesecake

PREHEAT OVEN TO 375° F (190° C)
9-INCH (2.5 L) SPRINGFORM PAN

Crust

1 cup	butter, softened	250 mL
1 cup	granulated sugar	250 mL
2	egg yolks	2
2 cups	all-purpose flour	500 mL
1 1/4 cups	ground almonds	300 mL
1/2 tsp	cinnamon	2 mL

Filling

3 cups	ricotta cheese	750 mL
1/3 cup	granulated sugar	75 mL
4	eggs, separated	4
1/2 tsp	almond extract	2 mL
	Icing sugar	

1. Make the crust: In a bowl, cream butter with sugar until fluffy; beat in egg yolks. Stir in flour, almonds and cinnamon until crumbly. Reserve one-third of mixture for topping. Pat remaining two-thirds of mixture onto bottom and sides of springform pan; chill.

2. Make the filling: In a bowl, beat ricotta with sugar until smooth; beat in egg yolks and almond extract. In a separate bowl, beat egg whites until stiff peaks form. Stir one-quarter of egg whites into ricotta mixture; gently fold in remaining whites. Pour into prepared crust. Crumble reserved crust mixture over top. Bake 50 to 60 minutes or until cake tester inserted in center comes out almost dry. Turn heat off; cool cheesecake in oven with door open. Chill. Serve dusted with sifted icing sugar.

Ferrara – New York

Serves 12

TIP

Substitute other cookie crumbs for graham. Buy cookies in bulk food department and grind into crumbs.

A beautiful sour cream web design can be added just before baking.

MAKE AHEAD

Bake up to 2 days in advance.

Freeze tightly wrapped up to 6 weeks.

FROM
Rose Reisman's Light
Vegetarian Cooking

Molasses and Cinnamon Cheesecake

PREHEAT OVEN TO 350° F (180° C)
8-INCH (2 L) SPRINGFORM PAN SPRAYED WITH VEGETABLE SPRAY

Crust

1 1/2 cups	graham cracker crumbs	375 mL
2 tbsp	packed brown sugar	25 mL
2 tbsp	water	25 mL
1 tbsp	vegetable oil	15 mL
1/2 tsp	ground cinnamon	2 mL

Filling

1 1/2 cups	extra-smooth 5% ricotta cheese	375 mL
1/2 cup	packed brown sugar	125 mL
1/3 cup	light cream cheese	75 mL
1/3 cup	light sour cream	75 mL
2	eggs, separated	2
2 tbsp	molasses	25 mL
2 tbsp	all-purpose flour	25 mL
1 tsp	ground cinnamon	5 mL
1 tsp	vanilla extract	5 mL
1/2 tsp	ground ginger	2 mL
1/4 tsp	ground nutmeg	1 mL
1/8 tsp	ground allspice	0.5 mL
2 tbsp	granulated sugar	25 mL

1. Make the crust: In a bowl stir together graham crumbs, brown sugar, water, oil and cinnamon. Pat mixture onto bottom and sides of prepared springform pan.

2. Make the filling: In a food processor or in a bowl, beat together ricotta, brown sugar, cream cheese, sour cream, egg yolks, molasses, flour, cinnamon, vanilla, ginger, nutmeg and allspice until smooth. In a separate bowl, beat egg whites until foamy; gradually add sugar, beating until stiff peaks form; fold into batter. Pour into crust.

3. Bake 45 to 50 minutes or until slightly loose just at center. Cool on wire rack. Chill before serving.

Marble Mocha Cheesecake

Serves 12

TIP

Serve with chocolate-dipped strawberries. Melt 2 oz (50 g) chocolate with 1 tsp (5 mL) vegetable oil. Dip the bottom half of the berry in chocolate.

Graham crackers or other cookie crumbs can be used for the crust.

Melt chocolate in microwave on Defrost or in a double boiler.

If instant coffee is unavailable, use 2 tsp (10 mL) prepared strong coffee.

MAKE AHEAD

Bake up to 2 days ahead and keep refrigerated.

Freeze for up to 6 weeks.

FROM
Rose Reisman's Enlightened
Home Cooking

PREHEAT OVEN TO 350° F (180° C)
8-INCH (2 L) SPRINGFORM PAN SPRAYED WITH VEGETABLE SPRAY

Crust

1 1/2 cups	chocolate wafer crumbs	375 mL
2 tbsp	granulated sugar	25 mL
2 tbsp	water	25 mL
1 tbsp	margarine *or* butter	15 mL

Filling

1 2/3 cups	5% ricotta cheese	400 mL
1/3 cup	softened light cream cheese	75 mL
3/4 cup	granulated sugar	175 mL
1	egg	1
1/3 cup	light sour cream *or* 2% yogurt	75 mL
1 tbsp	all-purpose flour	15 mL
1 tsp	vanilla	5 mL
1 1/2 tsp	instant coffee granules	7 mL
1 1/2 tsp	hot water	7 mL
3 tbsp	semi-soft chocolate chips, melted	45 mL

1. Combine chocolate crumbs, sugar, water and margarine; mix thoroughly. Press into bottom and up sides of springform pan.

2. In a large bowl or food processor, beat together ricotta cheese, cream cheese, sugar, egg, sour cream, flour and vanilla until well blended. Dissolve coffee granules in hot water; add to batter and mix until incorporated.

3. Pour batter into springform pan and smooth top. Drizzle melted chocolate on top. Draw knife or spatula through the chocolate and batter several times to create marbling. Bake for 35 to 40 minutes; center will be slightly loose. Let cool, and refrigerate several hours before serving.

Serves 12

No-Bake Pineapple Cheesecake

8- TO 9-INCH (20 TO 22.5 CM) PIE OR SPRINGFORM PAN SPRAYED WITH VEGETABLE SPRAY

1/4 cup	graham crackers	50 mL
1	can (8 oz [250 g]) crushed pineapple, with juice	1
1 tbsp	gelatin	15 mL
16 oz	ricotta cheese	
5	packets sweetener *or* 1/4 cup (50 mL) sugar *or* other equivalent sweetener	5
1 tsp	vanilla extract	5 mL
1 tsp	cinnamon	5 mL
	Slice fresh fruit to decorate	

1. Sprinkle graham crackers on sides and bottom of pan.

2. Drain 3 tbsp (45 mL) pineapple juice into a bowl. Set drained pineapple aside.

3. Combine gelatin and 1/4 cup (50 mL) boiling water; let stand until dissolved. Add to pineapple juice. Transfer mixture to blender or food processor.

4. Add ricotta, sweetener, vanilla, crushed pineapple and cinnamon; blend until smooth. Pour into pan and chill approximately 2 hours, until set.

FROM
Rose Reisman Brings Home
Spa Desserts

Serves 10 to 12

Miss Grimble's ABC Cheesecake

PREHEAT OVEN TO 350° F (190° C)
9-INCH (2.5 L) SPRINGFORM PAN

Crust

2 cups	graham wafer crumbs	500 mL
1/4 cup	melted butter	50 mL

Filling

1 1/2 lbs	cream cheese	750 g
1 cup	granulated sugar	250 mL
4	eggs, separated	4
1 tsp	vanilla extract	5 mL

Topping

2 cups	sour cream	500 mL
2 tbsp	granulated sugar	25 mL
1 tsp	vanilla extract	5 mL

1. Make the crust: In a bowl mix graham wafer crumbs with butter; pat onto bottom and up sides of pan. Chill.

2.. Make the filling: In a bowl, beat cream cheese with sugar until smooth; beat in egg yolks and vanilla. In a separate bowl, beat egg whites until stiff. Stir one-quarter of whites into cream cheese mixture; gently fold in remaining whites. Pour into pan. Bake 40 to 50 minutes or until just slightly loose at center. Remove from oven; increase oven heat to 475° F (240° C).

3. Make the topping: In a bowl stir together sour cream, sugar and vanilla. Spoon over hot cheesecake. Bake 5 minutes. Cool to room temperature on wire rack. Chill.

FROM
The Robert Rose Book
of Classic Desserts

Miss Grimble's - New York

Serves 10 to 12

Amaretto Cream Cheesecake

PREHEAT OVEN TO 325° F (160° C)
8-INCH (2 L) SPRINGFORM PAN

Crust

1 cup	graham wafer crumbs	250 mL
3 tbsp	butter, softened	45 mL
1 1/2 tsp	ground almonds	7 mL

Filling

1 1/2 lbs	cream cheese	750 g
1/2 cup	granulated sugar	125 mL
3	eggs	3
1/3 cup	sour cream	75 mL
2/3 cup	whipping (35%) cream	150 mL
1/2 cup	Amaretto liqueur	125 mL
	Toasted sliced almonds (optional)	
	Sliced fresh fruit (optional)	

1. Make the crust: In a bowl, blend graham wafer crumbs, butter and almonds until crumbs hold together. Pat onto bottom of pan. Chill.

2. Make the filling: In a bowl, beat cream cheese with sugar until smooth; add eggs, one at a time, beating well after each. Beat in sour cream. Stir in cream and Amaretto. Pour into crust.

3. Bake 1 hour or until just slightly loose at the center. Cool to room temperature on wire rack; chill. If desired, decorate with toasted sliced almonds or sliced fresh fruit before serving.

FROM
The Robert Rose Book
of Classic Desserts

Windows on the World – New York

Strawberry and Kiwi Cheesecake

PREHEAT OVEN TO 350° F (180° C)
8-INCH (2 L) SPRINGFORM PAN

8 oz	ricotta cheese	250 g
8 oz	2% cottage cheese	250 g
2/3 cup	granulated sugar	150 mL
1	large egg	1
1/4 cup	light sour cream	50 mL
2 tbsp	all-purpose flour	25 mL
1 tbsp	lemon juice	15 mL
1 tsp	lemon zest	5 mL
Crust		
1 1/2 cups	graham wafer crumbs	375 mL
2 tbsp	granulated sugar	25 mL
1 tbsp	margarine, melted	15 mL
2 tbsp	water	25 mL
Garnish		
2	kiwi fruit, sliced	2
1 cup	sliced strawberries	250 mL

1. Crust: In a bowl combine graham crumbs, sugar, margarine and water; mix well. Pat onto sides and bottom of cake pan; refrigerate.

2. In a food processor, combine ricotta and cottage cheeses, sugar and egg; process until completely smooth. Add sour cream, flour, lemon juice and rind; process until well combined. Pour into pan and bake for 35 minutes or until set around edge but still slightly loose in center. Let cool; refrigerate until well chilled.

3. Garnish cake decoratively with kiwi fruit and strawberries.

Tarts and Pies

Serves 8

FROM
The Robert Rose Book
of Classic Desserts

TIP

When melting chocolate over hot water, don't let the water boil and don't let the bowl touch the water – if the water boils or comes in contact with the bowl, the chocolate will scorch.

Strawberry Kiwi Cream Cheese Chocolate Flan

PREHEAT OVEN TO 375° F (190° C)
9- TO 10-INCH (23 TO 25 CM) FLAN PAN WITH REMOVABLE BOTTOM

Pastry

1 1/2 cups	all-purpose flour	375 mL
1/4 cup	granulated sugar	50 mL
3/4 cup	butter	175 mL
1 1/2 tsp	white vinegar	7 mL

Filling

2 oz	semi-sweet chocolate	60 g
1 tbsp	whipping (35%) cream	15 mL
8 oz	cream cheese	250 g
3 tbsp	icing sugar	45 mL
2 tbsp	milk	25 mL
1/4 tsp	vanilla extract	1 mL

Topping

2 cups	strawberries, halved	500 mL
2	kiwi fruit, peeled and sliced	2
2 tbsp	red currant or apple jelly	25 mL
	Toasted sliced almonds	
	Icing sugar	

1. Make the pastry: In a bowl stir together flour and sugar. With a pastry cutter or two knives, cut in butter to achieve a coarse crumb consistency. Sprinkle in vinegar, tossing with a fork. Form into a ball, wrap in plastic wrap and chill 30 minutes. Pat into bottom and sides of flan pan. Freeze 5 to 10 minutes. Bake 15 to 20 minutes or until golden. Cool on wire rack.

2. Make the filling: In a bowl, melt the chocolate over hot (not boiling) water, stirring until smooth. Remove from heat; stir in cream. Pour into crust; chill for a few minutes. In a bowl, beat together cream cheese, icing sugar, milk and vanilla until smooth. Spread over chocolate; chill a few minutes.

3. Before serving, decorate with strawberries and kiwi fruit. In a small saucepan, melt jelly; brush over flan. Garnish with almonds and dust with sifted icing sugar.

Sweet Sue Pastries - Toronto

Serves 8

TIP

You can make the pastry in a food processor if you prefer.

FROM
The Robert Rose Book
of Classic Desserts

Almond Pear Cream Tart

PREHEAT OVEN TO 375° F (190° C)
10- TO 11-INCH (25 TO 28 CM) FLAN PAN WITH REMOVABLE BOTTOM

Poached Pears

4 cups	water	1 L
2 cups	granulated sugar	500 mL
1 tbsp	grated lemon zest	15 mL
2 tbsp	lemon juice	25 mL
1 tsp	milk	5 mL
6	pears, peeled, cored and halved	6

Pastry

1 1/2 cups	all-purpose flour	375 mL
1/3 cup	icing sugar	75 mL
3/4 cup	butter	175 mL

Almond Cream

4 oz	almond paste	125 g
1/2 cup	granulated sugar	125 mL
1/2 cup	butter, softened	125 mL
2	eggs	2
1/2 tsp	vanilla extract	2 mL
1/3 cup	all-purpose flour	75 mL

Topping

1/2 cup	apple jelly	125 mL
2 tbsp	fruit liqueur, preferably pear	25 mL
1/4 cup	chopped nuts (optional)	50 mL

1. Poach the pears: In a saucepan bring water, sugar, lemon zest, lemon juice and milk to a boil; add pears, reduce heat to a simmer and cook 10 to 15 minutes or until pears are tender. Remove from heat; set aside.

2. Make the pastry: In a bowl stir together flour and icing sugar. With a pastry cutter or two knives, cut in butter until dough forms. Form into a ball. Pat into bottom and sides of flan pan. Bake 20 minutes or until golden. Cool in pan on wire rack.

3. Make the almond cream: In a bowl, beat almond paste with sugar until smooth; beat in butter. Beat in eggs and vanilla until smooth. Stir in flour until combined. Chill until ready to use.

4. Assembly: Spread almond cream over cooled crust. Drain pears, discarding syrup; slice thinly and arrange on top of almond cream. Bake 45 minutes or until almond cream is set. Cool on wire rack.

5. Make topping: In a small saucepan, melt jelly; stir in liqueur. Brush over tart. Sprinkle with nuts, if desired.

John Clancy's — New York

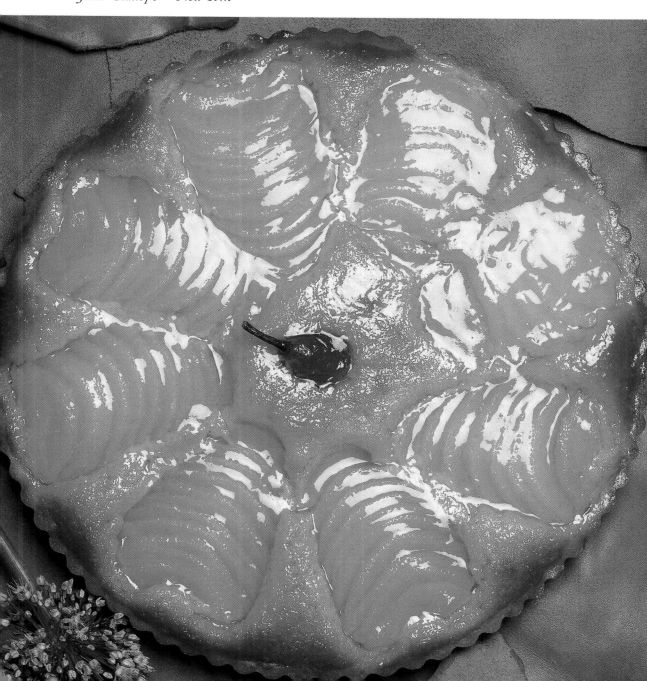

Lemon and Lime Meringue Pie

TIP

Do not use bottled lemon or lime juices — the pie will taste too tart.

Serve at room temperature or chill.

Do not overwork crust or it will toughen.

MAKE AHEAD

Bake early in the day.

FROM
Rose Reisman's Enlightened
Home Cooking

PREHEAT OVEN TO 375° F (190° C)
8- OR 8.5-INCH (2 OR 2.25 L) SPRINGFORM PAN SPRAYED
WITH VEGETABLE SPRAY

Crust

1 cup	all-purpose flour	250 mL
1/3 cup	granulated sugar	75 mL
1/3 cup	cold margarine *or* butter	75 mL
2 tbsp	2% yogurt	25 mL
1 to 2 tbsp	cold water	15 to 25 mL

Filling

1/4 cup	freshly squeezed lime juice	50 mL
1/4 cup	freshly squeezed lemon juice	50 mL
1 1/2 tsp	grated lime zest (about 2 limes)	7 mL
1 1/2 tsp	grated lemon zest (about 1 lemon)	7 mL
1	egg	1
1	egg white	1
1 1/3 cups	granulated sugar	325 mL
1 1/4 cups	water	300 mL
1/3 cup	cornstarch	75 mL
2 tsp	margarine *or* butter	10 mL

Topping

3	egg whites	3
1/2 tsp	cream of tartar	2 mL
1/3 cup	granulated sugar	75 mL

1. In bowl or food processor, combine flour and sugar; cut in margarine just until crumbly. With fork, gradually stir in yogurt and just enough of the cold water so dough comes together. Pat onto bottom and sides of pan. Bake approximately 18 minutes or until light brown. Raise heat to 425° F (220° C).

2. Meanwhile, in small bowl, combine lime and lemon juices, lime and lemon zest, egg and egg white; set aside.

Serves 6 to 8

TIP

This tart is best served the day it is made.

FROM
The Robert Rose Book
of Classic Desserts

3. In saucepan combine sugar, water and cornstarch. Bring to a boil; reduce heat to low and simmer for approximately 1 minute, stirring constantly, until mixture is smooth and thick. Pour a bit of the cornstarch mixture into the lemon–lime mixture and whisk together. Pour all back into saucepan and simmer, stirring constantly, for 5 minutes, or until thickened and smooth. Remove from heat. Stir in margarine. Pour into crust.

4. In a bowl, beat egg whites with cream of tartar until foamy; continue to beat, gradually adding sugar. Beat until stiff peaks form. Spread over filling. Bake approximately 5 minutes or until golden brown. Let cool.

Tarte Tatin

PREHEAT OVEN TO 350° F (180° C)
9- OR 10-INCH (23 OR 25 CM) PIE PLATE LINED WITH FOIL

1/4 cup	butter, softened	50 mL
7	Granny Smith apples	7
1 1/2 tbsp	granulated sugar	22 mL
1 1/2 tsp	cinnamon	7 mL
3 tbsp	butter	45 mL
1/3 cup	granulated sugar	75 mL
8	sheets phyllo pastry	8
2 tsp	melted butter	10 mL

1. Spread 1/4 cup (50 mL) butter over bottom and sides of prepared pan. Peel and core apples; slice each into 6 pieces and arrange in pan. In a small bowl, stir together 1 1/2 tbsp (22 mL) sugar and cinnamon; sprinkle over apples. In a small saucepan, melt butter with sugar; pour over apples.

2. Fold each phyllo sheet in half. Lay on top of apples one at a time, tucking in edges after each sheet. Brush top sheet with melted butter. Bake 30 minutes or until golden. Cool on wire rack 2 hours. Place serving plate on top of pie plate and quickly invert. Blot excess liquid with paper towels.

Patachou – Toronto

TIP

Use a pastry bag to pipe meringue onto hot filling for a fancier look.

You'll need 11 eggs in total for this tart.

Don't refrigerate meringue pies — if you do, the meringue will weep.

FROM
The Robert Rose Book
of Classic Desserts

Almond Lemon Meringue Tart

PREHEAT OVEN TO 375° F (190° C)
8- TO 9-INCH (20 TO 23 CM) FLAN PAN WITH
REMOVABLE BOTTOM, BUTTERED

Pastry

1/2 cup	butter, softened	125 mL
1/3 cup	granulated sugar	75 mL
2	egg yolks	2
1 1/4 cups	all-purpose flour (approximate)	300 mL

Almond Cream

1/4 cup	butter	50 mL
1/4 cup	granulated sugar	50 mL
1	egg	1
1 tbsp	grated lemon zest	15 mL
1/4 cup	ground almonds	50 mL

Lemon Filling

4	eggs	4
4	egg yolks	4
1/2 cup	granulated sugar	125 mL
6 tbsp	freshly squeezed lemon juice	90 mL
2 tbsp	butter, softened	25 mL

Meringue

5	egg whites	5
1/2 cup	granulated sugar	125 mL

1. Make the pastry: In a bowl, cream butter with sugar until fluffy; beat in egg yolks, one at a time. Stir in flour until dough forms; add more flour if dough is too sticky. Form into a ball, wrap in plastic wrap and chill 30 minutes.

2. Make the almond cream: In a bowl cream butter with sugar until fluffy; beat in egg and lemon zest. Fold in almonds.

3. Pat the chilled dough into bottom and sides of flan pan; spread with almond cream. Bake 30 minutes or until pastry is golden. Cool on wire rack. Increase oven to 475° F (240° C).

4. Make lemon filling: In a bowl set over hot (not boiling) water, whisk together eggs, egg yolks, sugar, lemon juice and butter; cook 15 minutes, stirring occasionally, or until thickened. Pour over almond cream.

5. Make the meringue: In a bowl, beat egg whites until soft peaks form; gradually add sugar, beating until stiff peaks form. Spoon meringue over hot filling, spreading to crust; with the back of a spoon, create decorative peaks and valleys. Bake 5 minutes or until meringue is golden. Cool on wire rack.

L'Hôtel - Toronto

Makes
12 servings

TIP

For a change, try lemon juice and zest instead of orange.

If desired, brush fruit with 2 tbsp (25 mL) melted apple jelly for a glaze.

MAKE AHEAD

Prepare a day before.

FROM
Rose Reisman Brings Home
Light Cooking

Tropical Fruit Tart

PREHEAT OVEN TO 400° F (200° C)
9-INCH (2 L) TART OR SPRINGFORM PAN SPRAYED WITH
VEGETABLE SPRAY

1 3/4 cups	2% yogurt	425 mL
2/3 cup	granulated sugar	150 mL
1/2 cup	light sour cream	125 mL
3 tbsp	frozen orange juice concentrate, thawed	45 mL
2 tbsp	all-purpose flour	25 mL
1 1/2 tsp	orange zest	7 mL
Crust		
1 1/4 cups	all-purpose flour	300 mL
1/4 cup	icing sugar	50 mL
1/3 cup	margarine	75 mL
3 tbsp	cold water (approximate)	45 mL
Topping		
3 cups	sliced fruit (kiwi fruit, mangos, papayas, star fruit)	750 mL

1. Crust: In a bowl combine flour with sugar; cut in margarine until crumbly. With a fork, gradually stir in water, adding 1 tbsp (15 mL) more if necessary to make dough hold together. Pat into pan and bake for 15 minutes or until browned. Reduce heat to 375° F (190° C).

2. Meanwhile, in a bowl, combine yogurt, sugar, sour cream, orange juice concentrate, flour and orange zest; mix well and pour over crust. Bake for 35 to 45 minutes or until filling is set. Let cool and refrigerate until chilled.

3. Topping: Decoratively arrange sliced fruit over filling.

TIP

You can make the pastry in a food processor if you prefer.

FROM
The Robert Rose Book
of Classic Desserts

Harvest Pie

PREHEAT OVEN TO 375° F (190° C)
9-INCH (2.5 L) SPRINGFORM PAN

Crust

1 1/2 cups	all-purpose flour	375 mL
1/3 cup	icing sugar	75 mL
3/4 cup	butter	175 mL

Filling

2 cups	sliced peeled apples	500 mL
1 cup	drained canned mandarin oranges	250 mL
1 cup	sliced peeled pears	250 mL
1 cup	raisins	250 mL
3/4 cup	granulated sugar	175 mL
1/4 cup	all-purpose flour	50 mL
1 tsp	cinnamon	5 mL
1/4 tsp	nutmeg	1 mL

Topping

1 cup	chopped pecans	250 mL
1/2 cup	all-purpose flour	125 mL
2/3 cup	granulated sugar	150 mL
1 tbsp	cinnamon	15 mL
1/2 cup	butter	125 mL

1. Make the crust: In a bowl stir together flour and icing sugar. With a pastry cutter or two knives, cut in butter until dough forms. Form into a ball. Pat into bottom and sides of springform pan. Bake 15 to 20 minutes or until golden. Cool in pan on wire rack.

2. Make the filling: In a bowl combine apples, mandarin oranges, pears, raisins, sugar, flour, cinnamon and nutmeg; toss until dry ingredients coat the fruit. Spoon into crust.

3. Make topping: In a bowl stir together pecans, flour, sugar and cinnamon. Cut in butter until crumbly. Sprinkle over filling. Bake 45 minutes or until fruit is tender. If topping browns too quickly, cover pan with foil. Cool on wire rack.

Dessert Peddler – Toronto

Serves 8

TIP

You can make the
pastry in a food
processor if you
prefer.

Chocolate Pecan Pie

PREHEAT OVEN TO 350° F (180° C)
9- TO 10-INCH (23 TO 25 CM) FLAN PAN
WITH REMOVABLE BOTTOM, BUTTERED

Crust

1 1/2 cups	all-purpose flour	375 mL
1/3 cup	icing sugar	75 mL
3/4 cup	butter	175 mL

Filling

3 oz	semi-sweet chocolate	90 g
2 tbsp	butter	25 mL
1 cup	corn syrup	250 mL
1 cup	granulated sugar	250 mL
3	eggs	3
1 cup	pecan halves	250 mL
1/4 cup	miniature chocolate chips (optional)	50 mL

1. Make the crust: In a bowl stir together flour and icing sugar. With a pastry cutter or two knives, cut in butter until dough forms. Form into a ball. Pat into bottom and sides of flan pan. Bake 15 to 20 minutes or until golden. Cool in pan on wire rack.

2. Make the filling: In a bowl, melt the chocolate with butter over hot (not boiling) water, stirring until smooth; set aside. In a saucepan, heat corn syrup with sugar until liquid; remove from heat and beat into chocolate mixture. Stir in pecans and, if desired, chocolate chips. Pour into crust. Bake about 45 minutes or until slightly loose just at center. Cool on wire rack.

FROM
The Robert Rose Book
of Classic Desserts

Gindi – New York

TIP

Chill the unbaked
crust for
30 minutes after
it's been patted
into the pan, if you
have the time.

FROM
The Robert Rose Book
of Classic Desserts

Apple Torte with Almond Cream

PREHEAT OVEN TO 400° F (200° C)
BAKING SHEET
9-INCH (23 CM) FLAN PAN WITH REMOVABLE BOTTOM, BUTTERED

Apple Filling

4	large Granny Smith apples	4
2/3 cup	granulated sugar	150 mL
1/4 cup	butter	50 mL
1/4 cup	Calvados *or* Amaretto	50 mL

Pastry

4 oz	butter	125 g
1/3 cup	granulated sugar	75 mL
2	egg yolks	2
1 1/4 cups	all-purpose flour (approximate)	300 mL

Almond Cream

1/4 cup	butter	50 mL
1/4 cup	granulated sugar	50 mL
1	egg	1
1 tbsp	grated lemon zest	15 mL
1/4 cup	ground almonds	50 mL
	Cinnamon	
	Granulated sugar	

1. Make the apple filling: Peel and core apples; slice thinly. Reserve one sliced apple for later. In a saucepan combine remaining sliced apples, sugar and butter; bring to a boil, reduce heat and simmer 3 to 5 minutes. Remove from heat; stir in Calvados. Pour mixture onto baking sheet to cool.

2. Make the pastry: In a bowl cream butter with sugar until fluffy. Add egg yolks, one at a time, beating well after each. Stir in flour to form a soft dough, adding more flour if too sticky. Using hands, press into bottom and sides of flan pan. Bake 10 minutes or until golden. Cook in pan on wire rack.

3. Make the almond cream: In a bowl, cream butter with sugar until fluffy. Beat in egg and lemon zest. Fold in almonds.

4. Assembly: Strain cooked apples, reserving liquid; pour apples into crust. Pour almond cream on top. Decorate with uncooked apples; brush with some of reserved cooking liquid. Sprinkle with cinnamon and sugar to taste. Cover with foil. Bake 25 minutes; remove foil and bake 10 minutes longer. Cool on wire rack.

L'Hôtel - Toronto

Wrenn's Ricotta Pie

Serves 8 to 12

FROM
The New Vegetarian Gourmet
by Byron Ayanoglu

Cooking for a film crew over a number of weeks while stuck in an exotic location (like the wilds of Newfoundland) means having to come up with new desserts every day. And when you run out of ideas — as I did — it's no laughing matter. An emergency phone call to Wrenn Goodrum in New York produced this lovely, no-bake cheesecake, reminiscent of Italian cannoli, without the fuss. It's not exactly diet material, but then again what proper dessert is?

For a creamier texture, use the smooth variety of ricotta.

**PREHEAT OVEN TO 350° F (180° C)
ROUND BAKING DISH (12-INCH [30 CM] DIAMETER),
GREASED WITH BUTTER**

1 cup	graham cracker crumbs	250 mL
1/4 cup	unsalted butter, melted	50 mL
1 tbsp	sugar	15 mL
2 cups	ricotta cheese	500 mL
1/4 cup	sugar	50 mL
3/4 cup	toasted slivered almonds	175 mL
1/2 cup	bittersweet chocolate chips	125 mL
1 tbsp	Amaretto liqueur	15 mL
1/2 cup	whipping (35%) cream	125 mL

1. In a bowl combine the graham cracker crumbs, butter and sugar; mix to a mealy, paste-like texture. Transfer the crumb mixture into the baking dish and press it down to cover the entire bottom (no need to do the sides). Bake for 10 to 12 minutes until slightly browned. Remove from oven and let cool down completely, about 45 minutes.

2. Meanwhile, in another bowl, combine ricotta and sugar; mix with a spoon to blend thoroughly.

3. In a food processor, grind half the toasted almonds (reserving the rest), until coarse meal. Add ground almonds to the ricotta mixture, and beat with a spoon to distribute. Add the chocolate chips and Amaretto. Beat well, until the mixture has become smooth, soft and thoroughly blended.

4. Add the whipping cream to a chilled bowl and beat until stiff; add cream to the ricotta mixture, folding it in gently but thoroughly.

5. Transfer mixture to the graham crust, smoothing it to fill the pan evenly. Garnish with reserved almond slivers, cover with plastic wrap and refrigerate for at least 2 hours until the cheese has stiffened. Serve cold.

Other Desserts

Makes 12 to 16 squares

Cream Cheese-Filled Brownies

TIP

This tastes like a low-fat Twinkie cupcake. Children and adults devour this dessert.

Double recipe and bake in a 9-inch square (2.5 L) baking dish 10 minutes longer or until slightly loose at the center.

When pouring batter, don't worry if there's a swirling pattern — the result will be attractive.

MAKE AHEAD

Prepare up to 2 days in advance. Freeze up to 4 weeks.

PREHEAT OVEN TO 350° F (180° C)
8-INCH (2 L) SQUARE BAKING DISH SPRAYED WITH VEGETABLE SPRAY

Filling

4 oz	light cream cheese, softened	125 g
2 tbsp	granulated sugar	25 mL
2 tbsp	2% milk	25 mL
1 tsp	vanilla extract	5 mL

Cake

1 cup	packed brown sugar	250 mL
1/3 cup	light sour cream	75 mL
1/4 cup	vegetable oil	50 mL
1	egg	1
1	egg white	1
3/4 cup	all-purpose flour	175 mL
1/2 cup	cocoa	125 mL
1 tsp	baking powder	5 mL

1. Make the filling: In a food processor or in a bowl with an electric mixer, beat together cream cheese, sugar, milk and vanilla until smooth. Set aside.

2. Make the cake: In a large bowl, whisk together brown sugar, sour cream, oil, whole egg and egg white. In a separate bowl, stir together flour, cocoa and baking powder. Add liquid ingredients to dry, blending just until mixed.

3. Pour half the cake batter into prepared pan. Spoon filling on top; spread with a wet knife. Pour remaining batter into pan. Bake 20 to 25 minutes or until just barely loose at center.

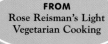

FROM
Rose Reisman's Light Vegetarian Cooking

Lemon Poppy Seed Loaf

**PREHEAT OVEN TO 350° F (180° C)
9- BY 5-INCH (2 L) LOAF PAN SPRAYED WITH
VEGETABLE SPRAY**

3/4 cup	granulated sugar	175 mL
1/3 cup	soft margarine	75 mL
1	egg	1
2 tsp	grated lemon zest	10 mL
3 tbsp	lemon juice	45 mL
1/3 cup	2% milk	75 mL
1 1/4 cups	all-purpose flour	300 mL
1 tbsp	poppy seeds	15 mL
1 tsp	baking powder	5 mL
1/2 tsp	baking soda	2 mL
1/3 cup	2% yogurt *or* light sour cream	75 mL
Glaze		
1/4 cup	icing sugar	50 mL
2 tbsp	lemon juice	25 mL

1. In a large bowl or food processor, beat together sugar, margarine, egg, lemon zest and juice, mixing well. Add milk, mixing well.

2. Combine flour, poppy seeds, baking powder and baking soda; add to bowl alternately with yogurt, mixing just until incorporated. Do not overmix. Pour into pan and bake for 35 to 40 minutes or until tester inserted into center comes out dry.

3. Glaze: Prick holes in top of loaf with a fork. Combine icing sugar with lemon juice; pour over loaf.

Serves 6 to 8

Fruit Salad with Ginger and Honey

The Chinese love simple fruit desserts. In Asia, a dessert called "icy bowls" (which resembles this fruit salad), is served over shaved ice, sometimes topped with coconut milk.

TIP

Feel free to add or substitute any fruits of your choice. Canned Asian fruits such as lychee and jackfruit will work very well in this recipe. And, of course, you can enrich it with coconut milk, if desired.

Sauce

1/4 cup	honey	50 mL
1 tsp	lime zest	5 mL
1 tsp	orange zest	5 mL
2 tsp	minced ginger root	10 mL
1 cup	apples cut into 1-inch (2.5 cm) cubes	250 mL
1 cup	cantaloupe cut into 1-inch (2.5 cm) cubes	250 mL
2 cups	honeydew melon cut into 1-inch (2.5 cm) cubes	500 mL
1 cup	pineapple cut into 1-inch (2.5 cm) cubes	250 mL
1 cup	seedless red grapes	250 mL

1. In a small bowl or pot, combine sauce ingredients; heat 30 seconds in microwave or until warmed through on top of stove. Set aside to cool.

2. In a mixing bowl, combine fruits; add sauce and mix well. Serve plain or with ice cream.

FROM
New World Chinese Cooking
by Bill Jones and
Stephen Wong

Carrot, Apple and Coconut Loaf

Makes
20 half slices

TIP

Grate carrots or chop and process them in food processor just until finely diced.

Chopped pitted dates can replace raisins.

MAKE AHEAD

Prepare up to a day ahead, or freeze up to 4 weeks.

PREHEAT OVEN TO 350° F (180° C)
9- BY 5-INCH (2 L) LOAF PAN SPRAYED WITH VEGETABLE SPRAY

2/3 cup	granulated sugar	150 mL
1/4 cup	margarine *or* butter	50 mL
2	eggs	2
1 1/2 tsp	cinnamon	7 mL
1/4 tsp	nutmeg	1 mL
1 tsp	vanilla	5 mL
1 1/4 cup	grated carrots	300 mL
2/3 cup	finely chopped peeled apples	150 mL
1/3 cup	unsweetened shredded coconut	75 mL
1/3 cup	raisins	75 mL
2/3 cup	all-purpose flour	150 mL
1/2 cup	whole wheat flour	125 mL
1 tsp	baking powder	5 mL
1 tsp	baking soda	5 mL
1/3 cup	2% yogurt	75 mL

1. In a large bowl or food processor, cream together sugar and margarine. Add eggs, cinnamon, nutmeg and vanilla; beat well. Stir in carrots, apples, coconut and raisins.

2. In bowl combine flour, whole wheat flour, baking powder and baking soda; add to batter alternately with yogurt, mixing until just combined. Pour batter into loaf pan; bake for 40 to 45 minutes or until tester inserted in center comes out clean.

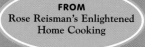

FROM
Rose Reisman's Enlightened
Home Cooking

Bread Pudding with Caramelized Pears

Serves 6 to 8

In the old days, bread puddings were an economy dish, simply made with stale bread and custard. But there's nothing humble about this recipe. The golden pear topping flecked with raisins transforms it into a special dessert fit for company.

TIP

Use homogenized milk to give this pudding an extra creamy texture.

Can't figure out the volume of a baking dish? Look for the measure-ments on the bottom of the dish or measure by pouring enough water to fill completely.

FROM
The Comfort Food Cookbook
by Johanna Burkhard

PREHEAT OVEN TO 350° F (180° C)
8-CUP (2 L) BAKING DISH, BUTTERED

6	slices egg (challah) bread *or* white sandwich bread	6
2 tbsp	butter, softened	25 mL
4	large eggs	4
1/3 cup	granulated sugar	75 mL
2 tsp	vanilla	10 mL
2 cups	hot milk	500 mL

Pear Topping

1/3 cup	granulated sugar	75 mL
2 tbsp	water	25 mL
4	pears, such as Bartlett, peeled, cored and sliced	4
1/2 tsp	nutmeg	2 mL
1/3 cup	raisins	75 mL
1/4 cup	sliced blanched almonds	50 mL

1. Trim crusts from bread; butter one side of each bread slice. Cut into 4 triangles each; layer in prepared baking dish, overlapping the triangles.

2. In a large bowl, whisk together eggs, sugar and vanilla. Whisk in hot milk in a stream, stirring constantly. Pour over bread.

3. In a large nonstick skillet over medium heat, cook sugar and water, stirring occasionally, until mixture turns a deep caramel color. Immediately add pears and nutmeg (be careful of spatters). Cook, stirring often, for 5 min-utes or until pears are tender and sauce is smooth. Stir in raisins; spoon evenly over bread slices. Sprinkle almonds over top.

4. Place baking dish in larger shallow roasting pan or deep broiler pan; add enough boiling water to come halfway up sides of dish. Bake in preheated oven for 40 to 45 minutes or until custard is set in center. Remove from water bath; place on rack to cool. Serve either warm or at room temperature.

Cocoa Roll with Creamy Cheese and Berries

PREHEAT OVEN TO 325° F (160° C)
JELLY ROLL PAN LINED WITH PARCHMENT PAPER AND SPRAYED WITH VEGETABLE SPRAY

5	egg whites	5
1/8 tsp	cream of tartar	0.5 mL
2/3 cup	granulated sugar	150 mL
1/2 cup	cake-and-pastry flour	125 mL
4 tsp	unsweetened cocoa powder	20 mL
1 1/2 tsp	vanilla	7 mL
	Icing sugar	
Filling		
1 1/4 cups	ricotta cheese	300 mL
1/4 cup	light sour cream	50 mL
3 tbsp	icing sugar	45 mL
1 1/4 cups	sliced strawberries and/or blueberries	300 mL

1. In a medium bowl, beat egg whites and cream of tartar until soft peaks form. Gradually beat in 1/3 cup (75 mL) of sugar until stiff peaks form.

2. Sift together remaining sugar, flour and cocoa; sift over egg whites and fold in gently along with vanilla. Do not overmix. Pour onto baking sheet and spread evenly. Bake for 15 to 20 minutes or until top springs back when lightly touched.

3. Filling: In a bowl or food processor, mix together cheese, sour cream and sugar until smooth. Fold in berries. Set aside.

4. Sprinkle cake lightly with icing sugar. Carefully invert onto surface sprinkled with icing sugar. Carefully remove parchment paper. Spread filling over cake and roll up. Place on serving dish. Sprinkle with icing sugar.

Makes 12 muffins

Banana Peanut Butter Chip Muffins

PREHEAT OVEN TO 375° F (190° C)
12 MUFFIN CUPS SPRAYED WITH VEGETABLE SPRAY

2/3 cup	granulated sugar	150 mL
3 tbsp	vegetable oil	45 mL
3 tbsp	peanut butter	45 mL
1	large banana, mashed	1
1	egg	1
1 tsp	vanilla	5 mL
3/4 cup	all-purpose flour	175 mL
3/4 tsp	baking powder	4 mL
3/4 tsp	baking soda	4 mL
1/4 cup	2% yogurt	50 mL
3 tbsp	semi-sweet chocolate chips	45 mL

1. In a large bowl or food processor, combine sugar, oil, peanut butter, banana, egg and vanilla; mix until well blended. In another bowl, combine flour, baking powder and baking soda; add to batter and mix just until blended. Stir in yogurt and chocolate chips.

2. Fill muffin cups half-full. Bake 15 to 18 minutes, or until tops are firm to the touch and cake tester inserted in the center comes out dry.

FROM
Rose Reisman's Enlightened
Home Cooking

Baked Peaches with an Almond Crust

There is no more magical time of year than peach season. It's full summer, the peaches are juicy enough to gag you if you eat them too fast and the days are finally long enough to allow for leisurely, al fresco dinners, where waiting 20 minutes for dessert is actually a pleasure. The almond paste can be prepared in advance, but the peaches must be stuffed and baked to order, and served hot directly from the oven.

FROM
Simply Mediterranean Cooking
by Byron Ayanoglu and
Algis Kemezys

BAKING DISH
PREHEAT OVEN TO 350° F (180° C)

6 tbsp	ground almonds	75 mL
2 tbsp	brown sugar *or* honey *or* maple syrup	25 mL
1 tbsp	softened unsalted butter	15 mL
2	large ripe peaches (not cling type)	2
1 tsp	softened unsalted butter	5 mL
	Chocolate ice cream and/or raspberry coulis	

1. In a small bowl, combine ground almonds, sugar and 1 tbsp (15 mL) butter, mixing with a spoon to form a paste.

2. Cut a ring around the peaches and neatly separate them in halves. Remove pits. Lightly rub 1 tsp (5 mL) butter all over the peaches to grease the surfaces. Put peach halves in baking dish, skin-side down. Heap a quarter of the almond paste into the pit cavity of each half.

3. Bake the peaches for 20 minutes. Serve (half a peach per portion) immediately, garnished with a dollop of ice cream and/or a smear of raspberry coulis.

Serves 10

TIP

Replace pears with apples, peaches or a combination.

Substitute other cookie crumbs for graham. Buy cookies in bulk food department and grind into crumbs.

MAKE AHEAD

Prepare crust, filling and topping up to 2 days in advance. Assemble just before baking.

FROM
Rose Reisman's Light Vegetarian Cooking

Pear and Raisin Custard Crumble

PREHEAT OVEN TO 350° F (180° C)
9-INCH (2.5 L) SPRINGFORM PAN SPRAYED WITH VEGETABLE SPRAY

Crust

1 1/2 cups	graham cracker crumbs	375 mL
2 tbsp	packed brown sugar	25 mL
2 1/2 tbsp	water	35 mL
1 tbsp	vegetable oil	15 mL
1/4 tsp	ground cinnamon	1 mL

Filling

3 cups	peeled diced pears (3 large)	750 mL
1/2 cup	raisins	125 mL
3 tbsp	packed brown sugar	45 mL
1/2 tsp	ground cinnamon	2 mL

Custard

1 cup	2% evaporated milk	250 mL
1/4 cup	granulated sugar	50 mL
2 tbsp	all-purpose flour	25 mL
1 tsp	vanilla extract	5 mL
1	egg yolk	1

Topping

1/2 cup	all-purpose flour	125 mL
1/3 cup	rolled oats	75 mL
1/4 cup	packed brown sugar	50 mL
2 tbsp	margarine or butter	25 mL
1/2 tsp	ground cinnamon	2 mL

1. In a bowl combine graham crumbs, brown sugar, water, oil and cinnamon. Press onto bottom and sides of prepared springform pan.

2. In a bowl combine pears, raisins, brown sugar and cinnamon. In a separate bowl, whisk together milk, sugar, flour, vanilla and egg yolk until well blended. In another bowl, combine flour, oats, brown sugar, margarine and cinnamon until crumbly.

3. Spoon pear mixture into crust. Pour custard mixture over. Sprinkle evenly with topping mixture. Bake 40 minutes or until pears are tender and custard is set.

Index

O

Oatmeal:
    date cookies, 19
    orange coconut cookies, 13
Old-fashioned carrot cake, 38
Orange:
    oatmeal cookies, 13
    sour cream apple cake, 32-33

P

Peaches:
    baked with an almond crust, 86
    blueberry cake, 30
Peanut butter:
    chocolate chip cookies, 22
    coconut-raisin granola bars, 18
Pears:
    almond cream tart, 62-63
    bread pudding with, 83
    pecan streusel cake, 34
    poached, 62-63
    and raisin custard crumble, 88
    sour cream orange cake, 32-33
Pecans:
    apple streusel cake, 34
    biscotti, 21
    chocolate chunk cookies, 15
    chocolate pie, 71
    topping, 69
Phyllo pastry, tarte Tatin, 65
Pie:
    chocolate pecan, 71
    harvest, 69
    lemon and lime meringue, 64-65
    See also Torte

Pineapple cheesecake, 54
Pine nuts, biscotti, 21
Poached pears, 62-63
Poppy seed, lemon loaf, 78
Pudding, bread, 83

R

Raisins, peanut butter granola
    bars, 18
Raspberries, chocolate mousse cake
    with, 45-46
Ricotta cheese:
    almond cheesecake, 50
    cheesecake, 74
Roll, cocoa with berries, 84
Rugelach, 8

S

Shortbread, 7
    See also Cookies
Sour cream:
    cinnamon coffee cake, 35
    orange apple cake, 32-33
    topping, 49
Strawberries:
    cocoa roll, 84
    cream cake, 24-25
    cream dacquoise, 29
    and kiwi cheesecake, 58
    kiwi cream cheese chocolate
      flan, 60
Streusel, 34
Sugar, superfine, 24
Swedish ginger wafers, 12

T

Tart:
  almond lemon meringue, 66–67
  almond pear cream, 62–63
  fruit, 68
Tarte Tatin, 65
Topping:
  coconut, 31
  meringue, 64–65
  pecan, 69
  sour cream, 49
  streusel, 34
Torte:
  apple with almond cream, 72–73
  See also Pie
Tropical fruit tart, 68

W

Walnuts, chocolate chunk
  cookies, 15
Whipped cream, about, 24
White chocolate:
  mousse cake, 43
  mousse layer cake with
    raspberries, 45–46
Wrenn's ricotta pie, 74

Z

Zucchini, chocolate chip banana
  cake, 41

If you've enjoyed the recipes in our "favorite" series, try our bestselling full-sized cookbooks.

Here's the book that established author Rose Reisman as a major force in the world of cookbook publishing. Now with more than 200,000 copies sold, *Light Cooking* proves that healthy eating doesn't have to be dull.

ISBN 1-896503-00-4

Everyone loves pasta. And here bestselling author Rose Reisman has created over 175 deliciously light pasta recipes. You won't believe how these pasta dishes can be so low in fat and calories — yet so full of flavor.

ISBN 1-896503-02-0

Everyone wants to provide their families with healthy, delicious meals. But these days, who has the time? You do! And Rose Reisman proves it in this collection of 175 light and easy recipes — all low in fat but full of taste.

ISBN 1-896503-12-8

Here's vegetarian cooking as only Rose Reisman can do it — imaginative, delicious and, unlike many vegetarian dishes, low in fat. A great book for today's families, with special appeal for "occasional vegetarians" who just want healthier meals.

ISBN 1-896503-66-7

Here's the ultimate book for pasta lovers, with over 100 recipes specially selected from the menus of top North American restaurants and adapted for home cooking. They're as simple to make as they are delicious. A must for every kitchen.

ISBN 1-896503-03-9

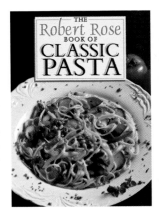

Go ahead — indulge yourself! Here's the ultimate collection of after-dinner delights, specially selected from the offerings of North America's top dessert chefs and adapted for home cooking. Over 100 recipes for the most scrumptiously satisfying desserts ever.

ISBN 1-896503-11-X

In *New World Noodles*, Bill Jones and Stephen Wong have created the next step in pasta books. Here's a fresh approach to mealtime, blending Eastern and Western flavors to give you a wide range of tantalizing dishes.

ISBN 1-896503-01-2

Take the best of Chinese cooking and put it together with an imaginative variety of North American ingredients. What have you got? The next step in Chinese cookbooks — *New World Chinese Cooking*. Easy, accessible and delicious!

ISBN 1-896503-70-5

Here's Mediterranean cooking at its best. Taste all the wonderfully fresh flavors of this sun-filled region, with over 100 dishes from Italy, France, Greece, Spain, Turkey and North Africa. They're as delicious as they are easy to prepare.

ISBN 1-896503-68-3

Byron Ayanoglu's *The New Vegetarian Gourmet* creates fast and easy culinary magic. These exquisite vegetarian recipes are a must for people who love great-tasting food but want all the benefits of vegetarian meals.

ISBN 1-896503-26-8

Johanna Burkhard's *Comfort Food Cookbook* brings you over 100 fast, easy recipes for the most comforting dishes you've ever tasted, fully updated for today's families. So relax. This is the kind of old-fashioned food that just makes you feel good.

ISBN 1-896503-07-1

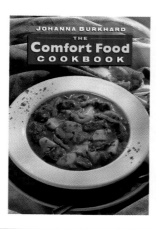
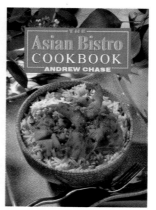

With *The Asian Bistro Cookbook*, Andrew Chase brings you all the best of China, Japan and Thailand — plus tantalizing dishes from the Philippines and Korea, as well as Vietnam, Indonesia and Taiwan. They're unusual and they're delicious.

ISBN 1-896503-21-7

AVAILABLE AT BOOKSTORES AND OTHER FINE RETAILERS

Just about everyone loves pasta. After all, there are few types of food that can be prepared in so many interesting ways. And that's what you'll discover in this book — over 50 pasta recipes, from classic comfort foods like macaroni and cheese to more exotic Asian-inspired noodle dishes.

ISBN 1-896503-74-8

Here's a book for all the people who love desserts, but worry about the fat and calories. Imagine being able to indulge, guilt-free, in luscious cheesecakes, pies — even chocolate desserts! Well, now you can. Over 50 great recipes with less than 200 calories per serving.

ISBN 1-896503-72-1

Whether for reasons of health or lifestyle choice, the fact is that more and more families are eating meatless meals. And that's why we've put together this special collection of over 50 sensational vegetarian recipes — each one so delicious, you'll never miss the meat.

ISBN 1-896503-67-5

Want something quick, easy and delicious? Then here's the book for you. Whether it's snacks for your kids, a light salad for lunch, or appetizers for dinner-party guests, you'll find just the right thing in this collection of 50 great recipes. They're winners every time.

ISBN 1-896503-51-9

Call it the most comforting type of comfort food — nothing beats a big bowl of hot soup or stew for pure, old-fashioned satisfaction. Here are over 50 outstanding recipes for these one-pot wonders. This book will be a popular addition to every family's kitchen.

ISBN 1-896503-69-1

What can you serve at mealtime that's guaranteed to please just about everyone? Chicken, of course! After all, chicken is lean and healthy; it's affordable and it's tremendously versatile. Here you get more than 50 terrific chicken recipes. A must for anyone who loves chicken.

ISBN 1-896503-53-5